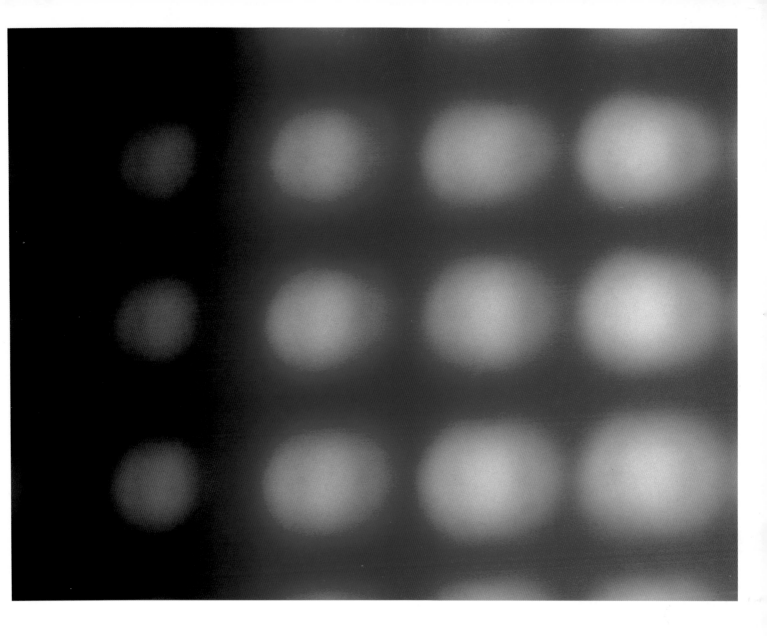

BRITISH PACKAGING | **DESIGN FOR TODAY'S CONSUMER INTERFACE**

BRITISH PACKAGING | **DESIGN FOR TODAY'S CONSUMER INTERFACE**

EDITOR Edward Booth-Clibborn

CREDITS

EDITOR
Edward Booth-Clibborn
BOOK DESIGN
Christian Küsters @ CHK Design Ltd
CO-ORDINATOR AND DESIGN ASSISTANT
Christie Grotheim
COVER AND DIVIDERS PHOTOGRAPHY
Paul Wesley Griggs

The captions and artwork in this
book are based on material supplied
by the designers whose work is
included. While every effort has
been made to ensure their accuracy,
'DESIGN FOR TODAY'S CONSUMER INTERFACE'
does not under any circumstances accept any
responsibility for any errors or omissions.

Printed and bound in Hong Kong.

Published and distributed in the United
Kingdom. Direct mail rights in Europe:
Internos Books Limited
12 Percy Street
London W1P 9FB
England

ISBN 1873968 99X

Distribution for the rest of the world:
Hearst Books International
1350 Avenue of the Americas
New York, NY 10019
United States of America

Distribution in the USA and Canada
rights reserved

CONTENTS

The old saw 'never judge a book by its cover' was for a long time entirely applicable to packaging design. Practicality came before presentation, and what was contained in the pack was always more important than the surface decoration. Those days are no more. Today, good packaging design can transform a tired product into a market leader overnight, while bad design can consign good stock to the supermarket incinerator. The progress made in all forms of graphic design over the last thirty years has played an important part in the current standing of British pack design.

But more significant still has been the rise of consumerism, more specifically the increasing demands of the consumer. Faced by more and more choice, consumers are no longer influenced to such an extent by a product's brand or advertising campaign; very often, they buy the packaging. Not only has packaging design become a sophisticated tool used by retailers to identify their products, it is also subtly appropriated by the consumers themselves as a way of expressing a lifestyle choice. This is seen in almost every sector of the market, as this book so clearly illustrates. Foods are packed not just to stand out on the supermarket shelf, but to add style to the dining-room table; soft drink cans are designed to convey a sense of mood as well as flavour; medicines are made to look wholesome and health-giving. Working alongside this recognition of the importance of visually attractive packaging is a more fundamental shift in design criteria. Where once the tactile qualities of a pack, including its ease of opening, were more or less ignored, today's manufacturers are asking designers to create containers that not only express the look and feel of their products, but also make them more accessible.

The work in this book shows the high standard of contemporary packaging design, and also gives some pointers to the future. It demonstrates the new interface between adventurous clients who are not afraid to commission imaginative designers, and the ways in which both clients and designers are responding to market demands. Above all, it shows that British packaging designers are still among the best in the world, and easily the most creative.

Edward Booth-Clibborn, 1996

PET SHOP BOYS
LIBERATION
THE E SMOOVE
& MURK REMIXES

PET SHOP BOYS LIBERATION

DESIGN GROUP
Dolphin
CLIENT/MANUFACTURER
Parlophone Records

The imagery for this sleeve was influenced
by and eventually taken from the video for this
song made and directed by Why Not Films.
The images consisted of 3D computer animated
spinning heads representing both of the Pet
Shop Boys. The spinning heads were transferred
to Quantel Paintbox where they were
integrated, their movement softened and their
colours enhanced, in order to create a stronger
visual for maximum standout on the shelf.

PET SHOP BOYS
YOUNG OFFENDER
THE JAM & SPOON
REMIXES

K-klass

Side A:1
Let me show you [Ktub mix].

Side A:2
Let me show you [Pharmacy dub].

Side B:1
1,2,3 [Sabres of paradise mix].

K-KLASS SINGLES
LET ME SHOW YOU / WHAT YOU'RE MISSING

DESIGN GROUP
Dolphin
CLIENT/MANUFACTURER
Deconstruction Records

K-Klass are a dance act who wanted to remain invisible. Unlike other acts, they wanted to be represented purely through their music and the imagery associated with it. In doing so, K-Klass broke the industry norm of having photographs of the act on the front of their sleeves. Therefore it was extremely important for Dolphin to come up with individual and distinctive visual imagery for each sleeve. Stock photography was used in these instances.

K-klass

What you're missing. A1. Klub mix. A2. Pharmacy dub. B1. Universal 94 mix. B2. Cream dub.

THE HED BOYS GIRLS + BOYS

DESIGN GROUP
Dolphin

CLIENT/MANUFACTURER
Deconstruction Records

For this particular single and its accom panying formats a handbag was used as the key visual image. Handbag is a term associated with the happy house music style of this track. The shot was taken by art photographers to reflect the look of a contemporary art installation. Dolphin deliberately chose a type style situated directly over the image - an application synonymous with the art movement.

TANITA TIKARAM I MIGHT BE CRYING

DESIGNER/ART DIRECTOR
Sammy Farrington
PHOTOGRAPHER
Jean Baptiste Mondino
DESIGN GROUP
Farrington Associates
CLIENT/MANUFACTURER
East West Records

As this was Tanita Tikaram's first release for some time, the designers wanted to re-introduce her to her audience with a more positive image. The clean, modern type and colour photography by Jean Baptiste Mondino were designed to complement the artist's personality and music, and to bring her image up to date. Some of the colour images used throughout the campaign suggested the more humorous and fun side of the artist's character.

TANITA TIKARAM.
I MIGHT BE CRYING.

7 4509-98900-2 5

YZ879CDX 4509-98900-2

LC 1557

 east west

TANITA TIKARAM.
I MIGHT BE CRYING.
FIVE FEET AWAY.
NOT WAVING BUT
DROWNING.

PRODUCED BY TANITA TIKARAM. WORDS & MUSIC BY TANITA TIKARAM EXCEPT TRACK THREE, MUSIC BY TANITA TIKARAM AND WORDS BY STEVIE SMITH. PUBLISHED BY BROGUE MUSIC/WCM EXCEPT TRACK THREE, PUBLISHED BY BROGUE MUSIC/WCM AND THE STEVIE SMITH ESTATE. 'NOT WAVING BUT DROWNING' COMMISSIONED BY THE BBC FOR THEIR TEXTS IN TIME-THE PICTURE IN THE POEM SERIES. TANITA TIKARAM IS AN ASGARD ARTIST. TRACK ONE IS TAKEN FROM THE FORTHCOMING ALBUM 'LOVERS IN THE CITY'. DESIGN BY FARRINGTON ASSOCIATES. PHOTOGRAPHY BY JEAN BAPTISTE MONDINO.

DESIGNER/ART DIRECTOR
Sammy Farrington
PHOTOGRAPHER
Anonymous
DESIGN GROUP
Farrington Associates
CLIENT/MANUFACTURER
East West Records

The image of the building of the Tyne
bridge, which was found amongst
a series of contemporary photographs,
was used to complement the tone and
content of Jimmy Nail's song, Big River.
The typography adds strength to the
package yet does not interfere with
the photographic image.

Jimmy Nail · Big River

1. Big River. 5.59 **2. Bitter and Twisted (Live Version).** 4.08
3. What Kind of Man Am I ? (Live Version). 5.32 **4. Big River (Radio Edit).** 4.17
All tracks written by Jimmy Nail. Published by Zomba Music Publishers Limited. Tracks one and four produced by
Jimmy Nail and Danny Schogger. Tracks two and three recorded by The Manor Mobile at Sheffield Arena, June 21st,
1995 and produced by Jimmy Nail. All tracks mixed by Jon Kelly. Mark Knopfler appears courtesy of Mercury
Records Limited for the world excluding the USA, and of Warner Brothers. Inc. for the USA only.
From the forthcoming album 'Big River'.

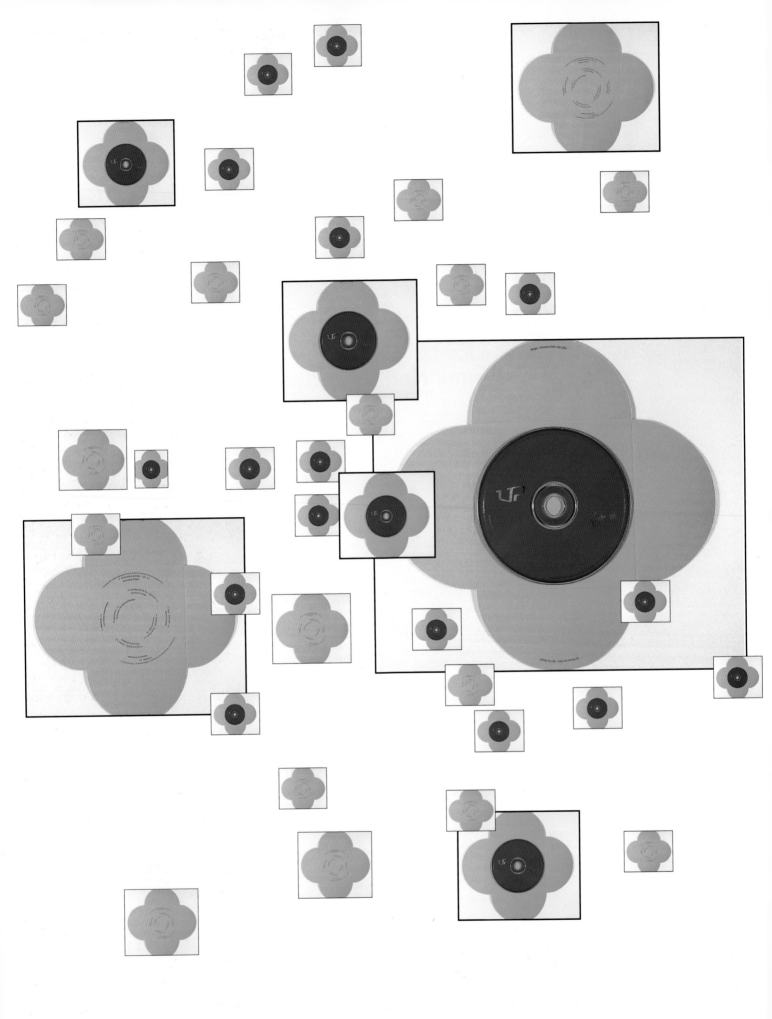

Up Sampler : March 1996

DESIGNER/ART DIRECTOR
Sammy Farrington
PHOTOGRAPHER
Sue Parker
DESIGN GROUP
Farrington Associates
CLIENT/MANUFACTURER
Polydor

As an artist who is passionate about her work, Yazz likes to get involved in every aspect of the music business, including the promotional side of things. The designers worked closely with her to create an identity for her One on One campaign which reflected her feelings about the songs on the album. Sue Parker's photographs were combined to create a multi-layered image, on the one hand open and revealing, on the other intense and introverted. The booklets unfold to reveal even more layering of images, with the songs' lyrics making up the final layer reversed out of the images.

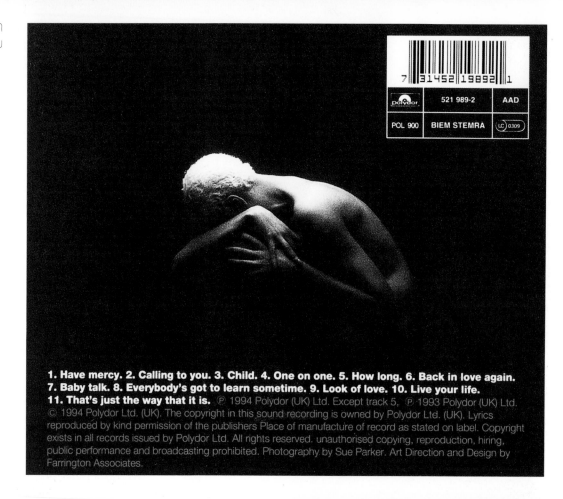

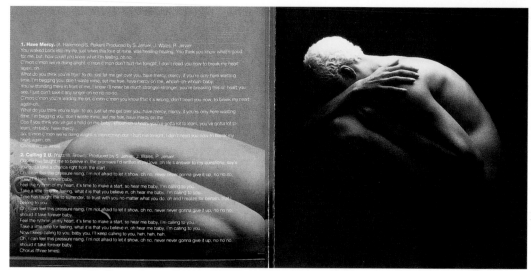

DESIGNER/ART DIRECTOR Yuki Miyake
DESIGN GROUP System Gafa
CLIENT/MANUFACTURER Trade 2

The last in the designer's high rises series,
the theme is concluded with the image
of high rises under the sea. The vibrant use
of colour, movement and surreal elements
relate well to the urban, spacey music.
The idea of transforming the ordinary
into the extraordinary, and in fact giving
something dull and dormant a sense
of life and excitement is something to
which this music's audience responds.
The strong concept and design have proved
successful as the band is on the rise.

DESIGNER/ART DIRECTOR
Yuki Miyake
PHOTOGRAPHER
Parker
DESIGN GROUP
System Gafa
CLIENT/MANUFACTURER
Rough Trade Records

System Gafa was commissioned by the
techno band, Spring Heel Jack, to design
their first single after seeing a book
produced by Yuki Miyake based on
J.G. Ballard's futuristic writings. The
book contains images of 'futuristic city
scapes' which the band felt suited their
music perfectly. So for their first single
the image of high rise Hackney council
estates were used. Changing the grey of
the flats into holiday brochure brightness
in her computer, the designer married
these images with Dead History fonts
designed by P. Scott Makela. The images
were then manipulated in Photoshop.

DESIGNER/ART DIRECTOR
Yuki Miyake
DESIGN GROUP
System Gafa
CLIENT/MANUFACTURER
Trade 2 Records

For their new single Spring Heel Jack wanted
a completely new look from their previous
releases. The designer used Darren O'Brien's
sliced photography as the bases for the
design, with the image echoing the layered
sampling sounds perfectly. For the track
called 'Wide as the Moon', the designer
manipulated the painting in Photoshop
to create the sphere shape which reinforces
the spacy, futuristic image. Yellow was
chosen for the logo to give greater prominence
to the image.

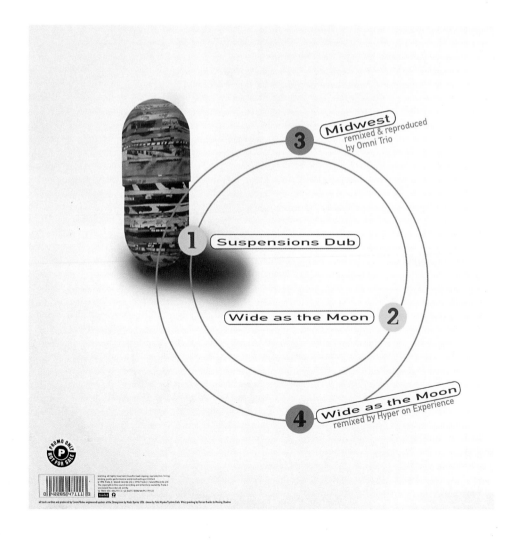

DESIGNER/ART DIRECTOR Yuki Miyake
PHOTOGRAPHER Parker
DESIGN GROUP System Gafa
CLIENT/MANUFACTURER Trade 2

When designing Spring Heel Jack's third
single, Sytem Gafa decided to continue
with the high rise theme to create an
identity that would reinforce recognition.
On this single, their usually cool, techno
music had a more bright up-beat sound,
a change reflected in the design's clunkier
comical feel. The striking colour is an
important element not only aesthetically,
but also for maximum shelf-appeal and
to provide easy recognition for DJs in
a nightclub atmosphere.

A 1 Lee Perry Part 1
    2 Lee Perry Part 3
AA 1 Lee Perry Part 2
    2 Lee Perry Part 4

ROUGH
TRADE

R3550

Photos by Parker Sleeve By System Gafa Yuki Miyake
P and C 1995 RoughTrade Records 66 Golborne Road London W10 5PS
Manufactured in the EC Distributed by Pinnacle

5 022781 003556

DESIGNER/ART DIRECTOR Yuki Miyake
PHOTOGRAPHER Bunsei Matsuura
DESIGN GROUP System Gafa
CLIENT/MANUFACTURER Q-Ring Records

Japanese ambient musician Kuri Suzuki also
makes art pieces. His visual work shares the
same theme as his music, namely archaeology,
which in turn inspired Yuki Miyake to use
the stone shape in her design. The front cover
image resembles fragments from a ruin found
in a museum, while Japanese characters based
on archaeology continue the theme on to the
actual disk for a complete, highly conceptual
package.

Kuri
Suzuki

QRI/01

Suzuki Kuri information
Q - RING Records
2-45-8 Green No.2
Shimoishihara
Cyofu Tokyo 182 Japan

Q-RING

produced by Shinohara Taro, Suzuki Kuri directed by Aoki Takaaki
mixed by Shinohara Taro, Suzuki Kuri recorded by Shinohara Taro, Aoki Takaaki,
Suzuki Kuri mastered at Tokyo CD Center recorded at Prefab Sonic, Green, Rail Side
instluments, programming and vox Suzuki Kuri co - programming Shinohara Taro
12 strings E. guiter - on 7 Aoki Takaaki
all composed by Suzuki Kuri

Soupy
Kuri Suzuki

Soupy

designed by System Gafa / Yuki Miyake
photography by Matsuura Bunsei
clay work by Suzuki Kuri
special thanks to
Hirokawa Takashi / Vivid sound Corporation,
Sayo, Kageyama Zulu

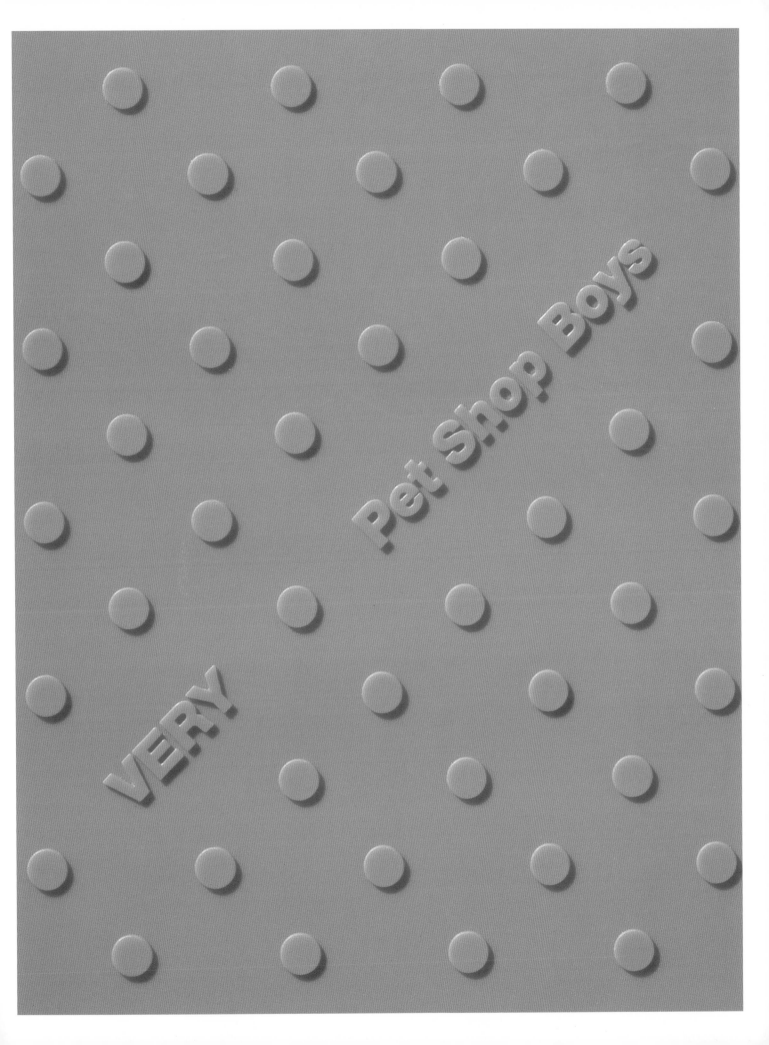

DESIGNER
Arthur Collin
ART DIRECTOR
Daniel Weil
DESIGN GROUP
Pentagram
CLIENT/MANUFACTURER
Parlophone

The strategy for the Pet Shop Boys'
new releases was to aim for a new
identity for a CD pack to make it
friendlier and more recognisable.
The solutions were interpreted in
a soft and hard version. The hard
case for the album Very, launched
in September 1993, provided the
up-front identity with its textured,
opaque orange jewel case.
This also provided a bank of colour
at point-of-sale along with an
eminently identifiable spine.
The fact that the pack was opaque
with a distinct texture provided
the client with an opportunity to
present the outer case as a product
itself. As a result, this became
part of the marketing/promotional
strategy. The soft version was
used for the limited edition release,
Very Restless, and for subsequent
singles.

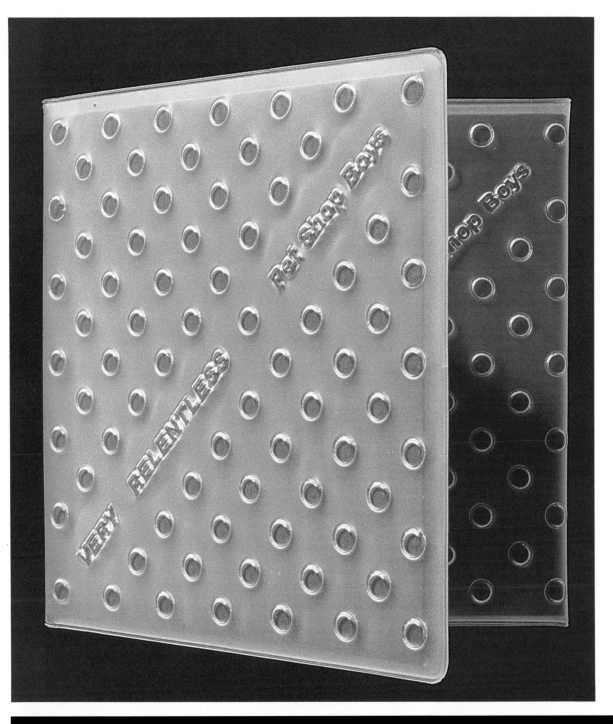
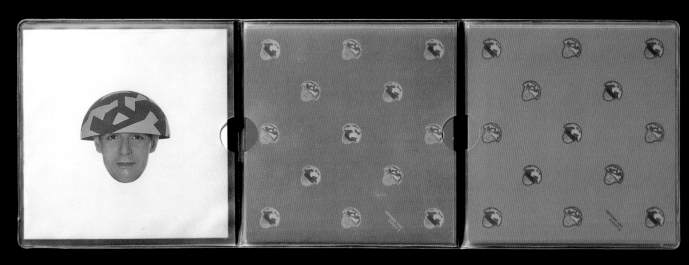

LIGHTNING SEEDS JOLLIFICATION

DESIGN GROUP Dolphin
CLIENT/MANUFACTURER Epic Records

The imagery for this sleeve was required to reflect the title of the album. It was decided that a strawberry with seeds made of a smiling child's face would fulfil this brief. To create that image a 25cm high strawberry was made out of fibre glass resin and photographed in sunlight to reflect warm natural lighting. Then a smiling five year old girl was photographed approximately 80 times from numerous different angles. The photographs of the strawberry and child were scanned into a Quantel Paintbox where each strawberry seed was replaced with the face of the child. Immense skill was needed to marry the angle of the child's face to that of each individual strawberry seed. The completed strawberry was then placed on a blue sky background surrounded by smaller, multicoloured strawberries to suggest a surreal, pop feel.

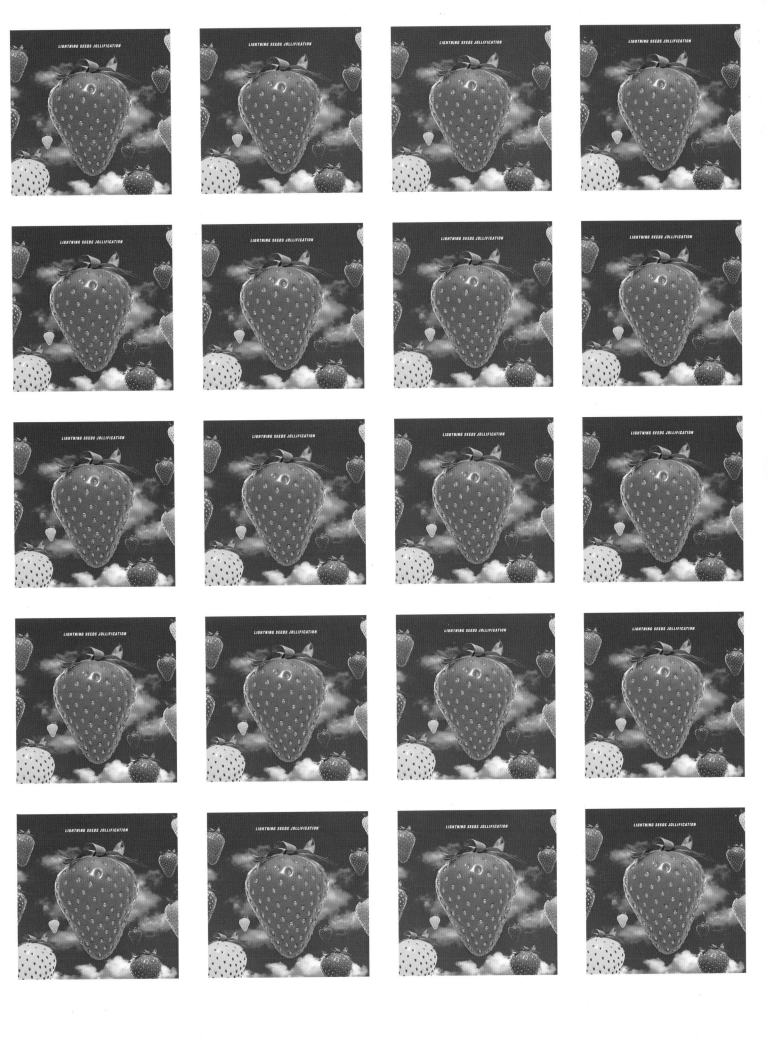

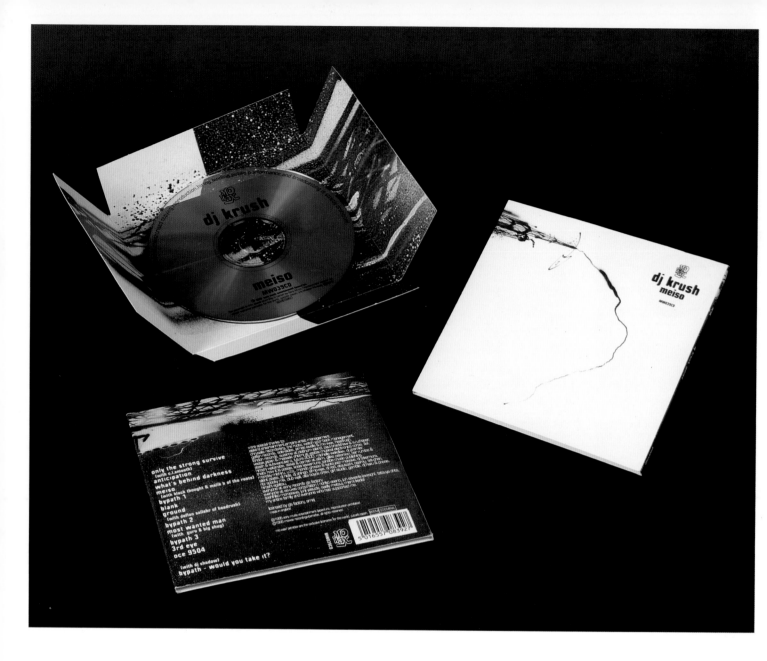

DJ KRUSH MEISO

DESIGNERS Ben Drury, Will Bankhead
PHOTOGRAPHER Barney Bankhead
ILLUSTRATOR Painting by Futura 2000
DESIGN GROUP Ben Drury & Will Bankhead
CLIENT/MANUFACTURER Mo-Wax Recordings

Mo-Wax Recordings is a vinyl-inspired label
for which the quality of its sleeve artwork
is a high priority. Their brief to the designers
was to create packaging which would retain
the qualities often associated with the vinyl
format: structurally sound enough to protect
the disc, yet with the same tactile qualities
as a record sleeve. The designers' solution
was to take away the jewel box quality of
CD packaging by removing the plastic barrier
between the consumer and the artwork, giving
people a desirable alternative to vinyl. In this
case, the package is based on an old-fashioned
cigarette pack. The protective layers of the

pack are maximised yet still offer the tactile
pleasure of a graphic unfolding slowly rather
than being pulled out in one swift movement.

Mysteries of BYZANTINE CHANT

KONTAKION

MYSTERIES OF BYZANTINE CHANT

DESIGNER/ART DIRECTOR Alex Smith
PHOTOGRAPHER Colin Gray
DESIGN GROUP Smith & Bull
CLIENT/MANUFACTURER
Philips Classics Productions

The rich, spiritual tones of plainsong have reached a broadening audience in the past couple of years. Creating a new approach in a competitive market packed with titles was a challenge. This cover was designed to be accessible to a wider market than the specialist classical one while still reflecting the nature of the music and emphasising its particular Byzantine style. Philips Classics wanted a look that was generally spiritual rather than religious and atmospheric while still relevant to the music. Above all, this cover needed to inspire the uncommitted chance buyer.

Smith & Bull felt that the ethereal multi-layered sound of Byzantine Chant could be best achieved with the use of photography. They sourced appropriate manuscripts for the photographer and suggested the Byzantine context of the music in their layering of colours, textures and simple typography.

DESIGNERS Ben Drury, Will Bankhead
PHOTOGRAPHER Mario Caldato Jr,
Paul 'Jazz' Thompson
DESIGN GROUP Ben Drury & Will Bankhead
CLIENT/MANUFACTURER Mo-Wax Recordings

These three packages fit in well with the
designers' approach to viable alternatives
to jewel boxes. Each one is a multi-folded
cardboard structure offering many protective
and printable surfaces. The 'lo-fi' image of
the artist is reflected in the graphic design
and uncoated design materials, and gives
him a strong identity in his own right.

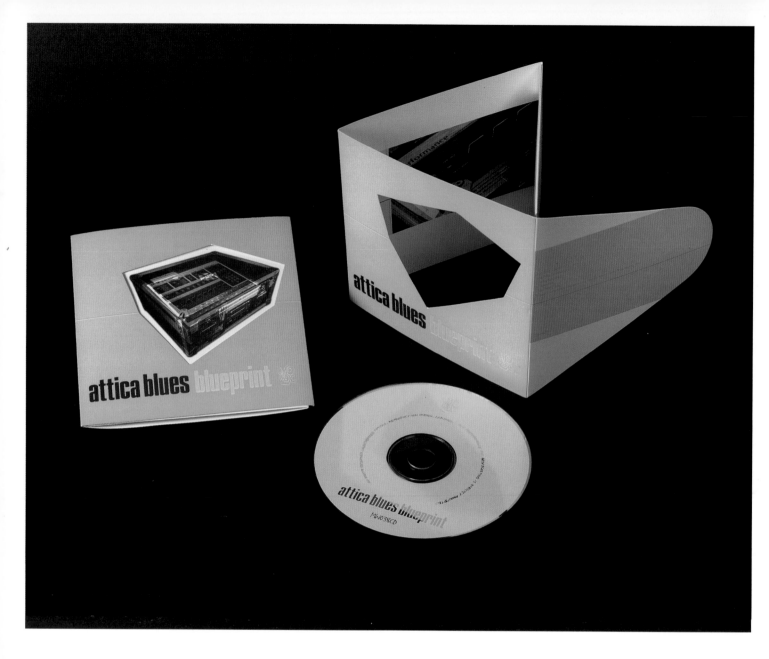

ATTICA BLUES BLUEPRINT

DESIGNERS Ben Drury, Will Bankhead
PHOTOGRAPHER Barney Bankhead
DESIGN GROUP Ben Drury & Will Bankhead
CLIENT/MANUFACTURER Mo-Wax Recordings

This is another variation of a multi-folding
cardboard structure which has been used to
provide layers of protection for the product.
The die-cut reveals the inner layers which
emphasise the montage of the drum machine
which, in turn, represents the blueprint of
the sound in this recording.

JOHNNY BAZOOKATONE GAME SOFTWARE

DESIGNER/ART DIRECTOR James Glover
DESIGN GROUP Fluid
CLIENT/MANUFACTURER US Gold

The character Johnny Bazookatone was created by Arc Developers in conjunction with US Gold. As US Gold needed to portray Johnny in a different style from their usual illustrative formats, Fluid were approached to create an image for the character. The designers decided to base the whole campaign around the stylish 3D rendered logo that the team came up with after watching the initial ideas of the platform game, then introduced the character later, without using the obvious screenshots of the game. The finished result was the new star's logo: Johnny's star. This is used throughout the game, in the opening sequences of each level, on packaging for all formats, and in the ad campaign using the line 'The birth of a star'.

The logo lent itself very well to the limited edition packaging; the inner ring encases the CD and manual, and the star points create stability on the shelves. The prototype case was made out of magenta plastic with white and blue finish on the star. Stacking the product in the delivery boxes and on the shelves in the stores proved problematical. The solution to this came from using a jigsaw effect on the back of the packaging so they would not slide around, get damaged or look untidy on the shelves.

DESIGNER/ART DIRECTOR
Yuki Miyake
PHOTOGRAPHER
Jo Agis
DESIGN GROUP
System Gafa
CLIENT/MANUFACTURER
Swivel Films

Swivel is a video production
company producing promotional
music videos. System Gafa were
commissioned to design two
different covers for their
showreels: the first for dance
music, the second for independent
music. Most designs for
showreels simply feature 'grabs'
or text. To create a unique
solution Yuki Miyake decided
to use the photography of Jo Agis,
who collaborates on Swivel's
animated promos. Agis provided
images of plastic turtles,
monkeys, stars, and a toy with
a gasmask. These were scanned
into a computer and manipulated
in Photoshop to create
a distinctive result.

Too Funky Reel

Featuring :
I Want More   *Megamix*
China Black   *Somewhere*
Alysha Warren   *I'm So In Love*
West End   *I Love Rules*
M - People   *Moving On Up*
China Black   *Searching*
De De   *Party*

" I Want More " Megamix Features clips from :
Wet Wet Wet Omar James Bob Geldof
A Guy Called Gerald Utah Saints Bass-O-Matic
Heroes Del Silencio Pasedenas M-People
Jesus&The Mary Chain Martha Wash
808 State and Squeeze

Also available : Faster Faster Reel
with Teenage Fanclub Squeeze
Jesus & Mary Chain Utah Saints etc˚

For copies of these and promos in Megamix contact Avril at Swivel
Swivel Films
4th Floor, 23 Denmark Street, London WC2H 8NA
tel 0171 240 4485 fax 0171 240 4486

SWIVEL

JOHN CLAYTON
SHOWREEL 2

Faster Faster Reel

Featuring :
Teenage Fanclub *Sparkeys Dream*
Squeeze *Third Rail*
Jesus & Mary Chain *Blues From A Gun*
Utah Saints *Believe In Me*
Taucher *Infinity*
I Want More *Megamix*

For copies of these and promos in Megamix
contact Avril at Swivel
Swivel Films
4th Floor, 23 Denmark Street, London WC2H 8NA
tel 0171 240 4485 fax 0171 240 4486

" I Want More " Megamix
Features clips from :
Wet Wet Wet Omar James
Bob Geldof A Guy Called Gerald
Utah Saints Bass-O-Matic
Heroes Del Silencio Pasedenas
M-People Jesus&The Mary Chain
Martha Wash 808 State
and Squeeze
Also available :Too Funkey Reel
with China Black Alysha Warren
M-People etc˙

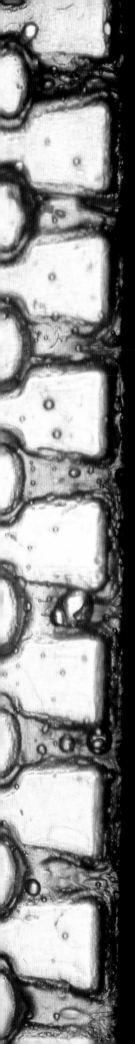

DESIGNER/ART DIRECTOR Ian Wills
DESIGN GROUP Clarks Shoes
In-House Design Group
CLIENT/MANUFACTURER
Clarks Shoes Childrens Division

Clarks Sunstone is a range of shoes made
of natural tan, brown, and burgundy
leathers aimed at seven to eight-year-old
girls. The brief called for packaging and
point-of-sale material, using a strong
golden sun motif that had already been
developed by the children's shoe design
team for use on the heel of the shoe.
A colour photocopy of the sun was used
to strengthen and make the image more
graphic. This was then superimposed over
a bright orange pencil-textured background
to give an ethnic feel relating back to the
shoes.Kraft corrugated bases with brightly
coloured lids and tissue paper form the

outer packaging for the product, while the same
is used for the smaller pot-pourri. These boxes,
together with some small showcards, form the
point-of-sale material.

CLARKS FOOTBALL BOOTS

DESIGNER Nick Reeve
ART DIRECTOR Ian Wills
ILLUSTRATOR Ron Mercer
DESIGN GROUP Clarks Shoes
In-House Design Group
CLIENT/MANUFACTURER
CICA, CJ Clark International

CICA Blades are a totally new concept in football boot sole technology. They are the result of a joint venture between CICA and an Australian entrepreneur who owned the idea and the Blades name.
The brief called for an identity to cover packaging, point-of-sale material, product badging, product hang-tags and leaflets. A badge was developed using the existing Blades logostyle with the CICA brandname and stripes to form a strong link to the graphic imagery of football shirts. The badge formed the basis of the identity and was

combined with technical information and product line-drawings that were spot-varnished on a matt laminated background to convey the boots' high specification and modernity. The product has now become highly sought after, especially amongst budding young footballers of the future.

DESIGNERS Victor Liew, Judi Green
ART DIRECTOR Judi Green
PHOTOGRAPHER James Wedge
DESIGN GROUP The Green House
CLIENT/MANUFACTURER Debenhams plc

With the packaging for Debenhams hosiery looking dated, The Green House was commissioned to reposition and repackage a range totalling up to 50 lines. The Opaque range, consisting of ten products, was specifically targeted at the young consumer. The Green House were briefed to reinforce the quality, value and wide range Debenhams offer in a highly competitive and active market. Unlike other own brand outlets, Debenhams also stock a wide range of branded products such as Aristoc, Pretty Polly and Wolford and therefore have to compete in a tough environment.

With a target market of 15 to 30-year-olds, the design objectives were to clarify the range, make selection easy and identify quality levels in the sub-ranges with the clear communication of specific product benefits. The aim was to create a strong brand design that would properly reflect Debenhams' personality and proposition, and thus build a closer relationship with the consumer. As the product is displayed out of the pack, the final design incorporates a strong Debenhams umbrella branding, uses a distinctive contemporary look, and features solarised prints with textured images to reflect the feel of the product.

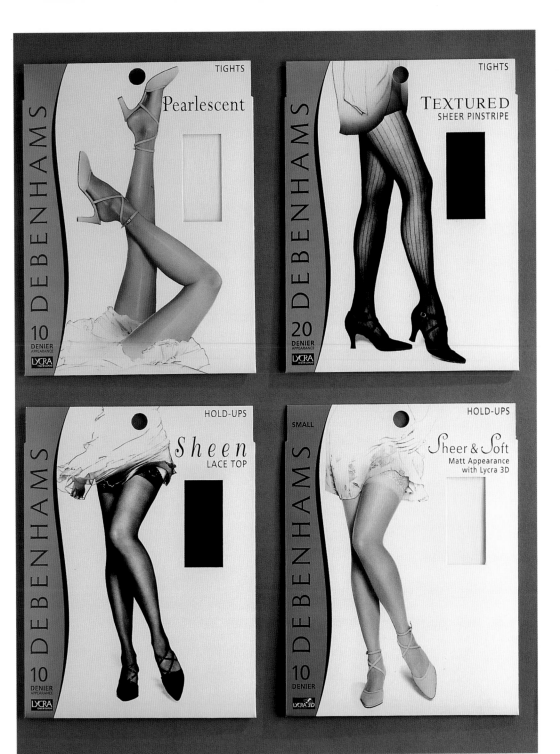

DESIGNERS Brian Green,
Judi Green, James Bell
ART DIRECTOR Judi Green
PHOTOGRAPHER James Wedge
DESIGN GROUP The Green House
CLIENT/MANUFACTURER Debenhams plc

As part of The Green House's commission
to reposition and repackage Debenhams'
range of up to 50 lines, this final design
for the Broadfold range uses a unique
combination of black and white
photography and hand coloured
illustration to create a striking image
in a highly competitive environment.

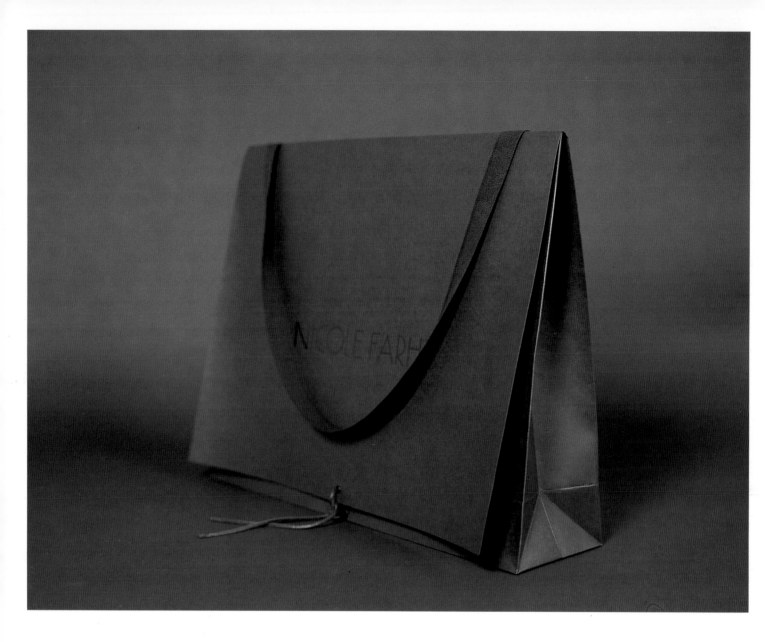

DESIGNER/ART DIRECTOR Valerie Wickes
DESIGN GROUP Din Graphics
CLIENT/MANUFACTURER Nicole Fahri

Nicole Fahri designs clothing that is both
beautiful and wearable. Her new womenswear
label, Black on Black, uses exquisite fabrics
in a dramatic monotone palette. Black on Black
is positioned slightly higher in the market place
than the main Nicole Fahri label. The collection
is sold within the flagship Nicole Fahri store
in Bond Street. To launch the label, and to set
Black on Black apart from Nicole Fahri, a sleek
new range of packaging and carrier bags were
designed. The use of textures in the packaging
echo the quality of the collection. Matt black
paper is used for the bags, black gloss foil for
the typography and black leather ties are used
to detail closure and handles across the range.
This portfolio bag is one of a set of Black on
Black bags designed to carry tailored suits
or jackets.

BRUCE OLDFIELD CARRIER BAGS

DESIGNER Bruce Duckworth, Geoff Halpin
ART DIRECTOR
Bruce Duckworth, David Turner
ILLUSTRATOR John Geary
DESIGN GROUP Turner Duckworth
CLIENT/MANUFACTURER
Bruce Oldfield Ready-To-Wear

Bruce Oldfield's name has become
synonymous with international couture
fashion. In launching his first ready-to-
wear collection, he was determined not
to lose any of the cachet associated
with his name. As fashion designers'
names and logos have become devalued
by over-use, Turner Duckworth wanted to
avoid an obvious or overblown solution.
The logo and brand name have been
interpreted in a subtle, almost codified
fashion for the Mayfair shop's carrier bag.
Only those in the know will recognise it.

SOCK SHOP RANGES

DESIGNERS Ruth Waddingham, David Beard
ART DIRECTOR Mark Wickens
PHOTOGRAPHERS
Robin Broadbent, Max Bradley
DESIGN GROUP Wickens Tutt Southgate
CLIENT/MANUFACTURER Sock Shop Ltd

Wickens Tutt Southgate was charged with the mission of emphasising Sock Shop's status as an authority in its sector positioned as inspiring, fun, friendly, highly contemporary, direct and confident. The design solution provides a clearly branded communication system for all copy in a hierarchy deemed relevant by the consumer, while using photography of abstract objects to communicate the main product benefit and the feel of the product - soft shiny objects for soft shiny tights, for example. An androgynous character moves among the objects on the pack, providing personality without depicting lifestyle. The four ranges were segmented by differing, unique, elliptical pack structures and by colour: monochrome for Essentials, an explosion of colour for Inspirations, sensual black and metallics for Luxuries, and the avant garde Showstoppers range. Clear packaging was used allowing the product to speak for itself.

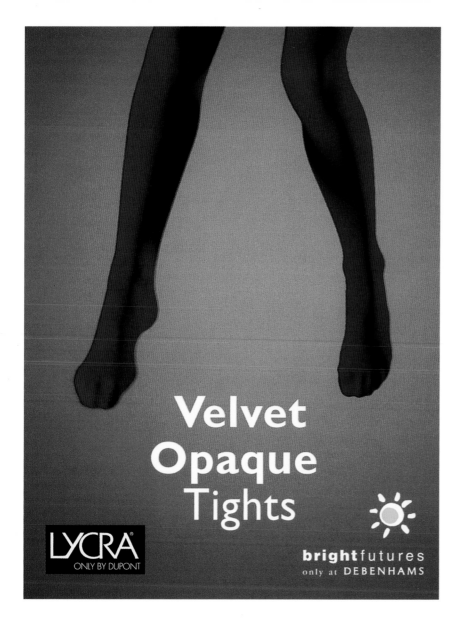

DEBENHAMS TIGHTS RANGE

DESIGNERS David Richmond, David Gray
ART DIRECTOR David Richmond
PHOTOGRAPHER Andrew Hall
DESIGN GROUP David Richmond Associates
CLIENT/MANUFACTURER Debenhams plc

The packaging for Debenhams' large range
of tights for girls needed to be redesigned
because the photography was dated and
confusion had been caused by a lack of coding
within a range encompassing both differences
in age groups and in styles of tights. The
brightly coloured backgrounds of the shots
keep the design clean and form a coding
to differentiate the various styles of tights.
The simplicity of the design allows
the product to be seen clearly, and the
information to be communicated without
confusion.

DESIGNERS Nik Daughtry, Jon Daughtry
DESIGN GROUP DED Associates
CLIENT/MANUFACTURER Ted Baker Shirts Ltd

Commissioned by Ted Baker, the shirt specialist, DED Associates' initial brief was to produce a pastiche of a 1950s soap box. The box was to be used for packaging, window displays and point-of-sale material in stores throughout the UK and in franchises further afield. Using the styles of a variety of well known brands DED expanded the brief to include six boxes rather than just one. Each box conveys its own recognisable brand name along with slogans such as 'LUK - with an unbeatable fashion softener', 'SHURTZ - sure do Dazzle' and 'TED - give Ted the window test', all produced under the name of 'Doctor & Scramble'. The full message becomes apparent when the six boxes are displayed together. It reads 'TED BAKER SHURTZ LUK REAL SWELL'. The boxes were screen-printed by hand and given a less than perfect finish for authenticity.

JOHN PARTRIDGE CLOTHING PACKAGING

DESIGNER/ART DIRECTOR Kathy Miller
PROJECT DIRECTOR Siân Sutherland
ILLUSTRATOR Geoff Appleton,
DESIGN GROUP Miller Sutherland
CLIENT/MANUFACTURER John Partridge

In a market notorious for short cuts and
cheap materials, John Partridge pride
themselves on the quality of their country
coats. Their brief to Miller Sutherland
was to create packaging which reflected
this attention to detail and would help
them differentiate between their general
country coats, their professional range
and the planned launch of a coastal line.
The designers created a core brand identity
which works across the three categories:
Country, Specialist and Britannia K.
This identity clearly conveys the company's
selling proposition, Handmade in England.
A special envelope was also created which
contains a guarantee card, fabric information,
care leaflets and information about the
John Partridge philosophy. The second phase
of the branding involved its implementation
across other media: carrier bags, woven
labels, accessories, signage and stationery.

DESIGNER Allison Miguel
ART DIRECTOR Mark Wickens
PHOTOGRAPHER Tim Platt
DESIGN GROUP Wickens Tutt Southgate
CLIENT/MANUFACTURER BHS

Men's underwear has increasingly
become part of the designer fashion
market. The most renowned menswear
designers are now often best known
for the smaller items in their portfolio:
'a pair of Calvin Kleins' has almost
become a generic term.
BHS needed to ensure that the evolving
and ever more aspirational needs of its
own target audience were met.
They briefed Wickens Tutt Southgate
to design the Men's Essentials range
to appeal not only to men, but also and
more frequently, to their wives and
girlfriends.
All of the consumers' aspirations were
met through use of evocative, monochromatic photography, in a style clearly
borrowed from the world of high fashion
as opposed to the world of department
stores. Yet the product, not the model,
is the hero. Meanwhile the bar around
which the models are posing provides
a no-nonsense, clear and simple
information system. It enables swift
decision-making while simultaneously
creating a very powerful billboard effect
throughout the category.

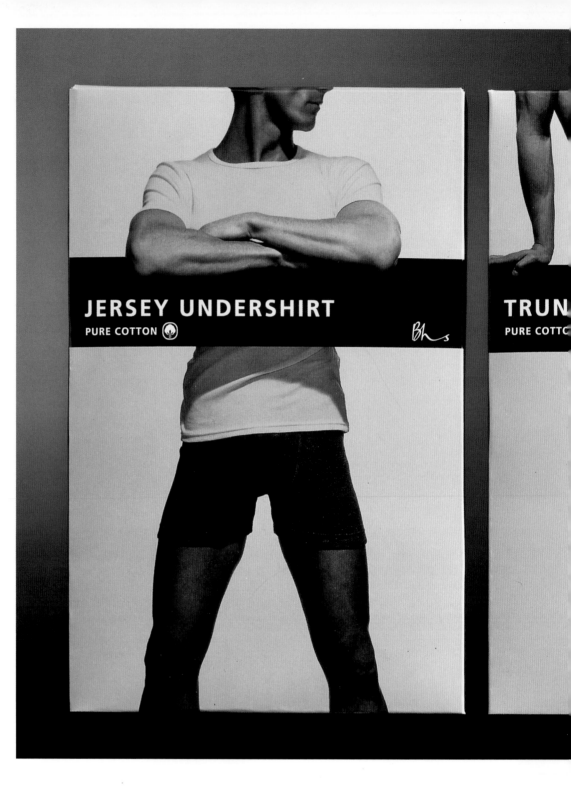

JERSEY UNDERSHIRT
PURE COTTON

TRUN
PURE COTTO

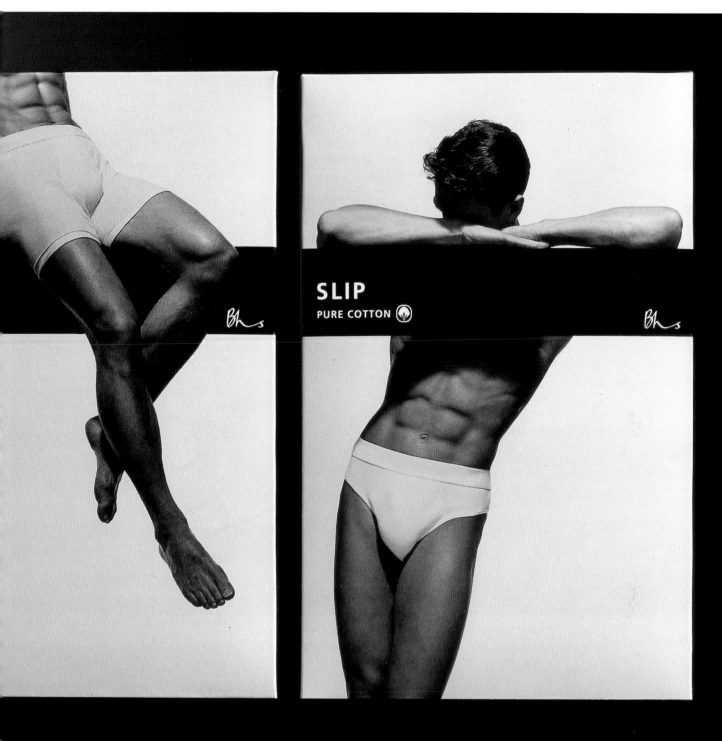

SLIP
PURE COTTON

FABRIS LANE SUNGLASSES

DESIGNER Victoria Fenton
ART DIRECTOR Steve Hutton
DESIGN GROUP Hutton & Partners
CLIENT/MANUFACTURER
Fabris Lane International Ltd

Two of the design requirements for this range
of sunglasses sold in supermarkets were to
deter pilfering and to demonstrate that the price
included a quality case and lens cleaning cloth.
Hutton & Partners created the pack shape and the
concept of a permanently fixed cord, which allows
the glasses to be tried on. The pack has a cut out
on the reverse to allow the lens cloth to be seen
and touched. The pillow pack also acts as a support
for the glasses, displaying them at the same
angle as when worn. Hutton & Partners created
the product brand name, Apollo, in homage to
the Greek god of the sun. The products are grouped
into one range for children and another for adults.

Gossard
ultrabra
PERFECTION™

denim plunge bra

THE ULTIMATE CLEAVAGE
with ultimate comfort™

GOSSARD ULTRABRA PERFECTION

DESIGNER Ashley Carter
ART DIRECTOR Mark Wickens
PHOTOGRAPHER Peggy Sirota
DESIGN GROUP Wickens Tutt Southgate
CLIENT/MANUFACTURER Gossard

The Gossard Ultrabra Perfection is a direct
competitor to the Playtex Wonderbra.
Traditionally, cleavage enhancing bras have
been positioned as glamour wear for parties
and night-time, worn by women for men and
not known for their comfort.
To keep ahead, Gossard not only introduced
a wide range of products in a variety of
styles, colours and fabrics, but created a
bra comfortable enough to wear all day long.
The new packaging range projects a product
that is implicitly comfortable, that can be
worn with confidence by women for women,
that is sexy yet not tarty.

A tight crop concentrates on the product and
the model's expression with bold branding
holding the eye on the cleavage. A variety of
poses and strong background colours create
effective product differentiation, keeping
the feel of the range light yet glamorous.

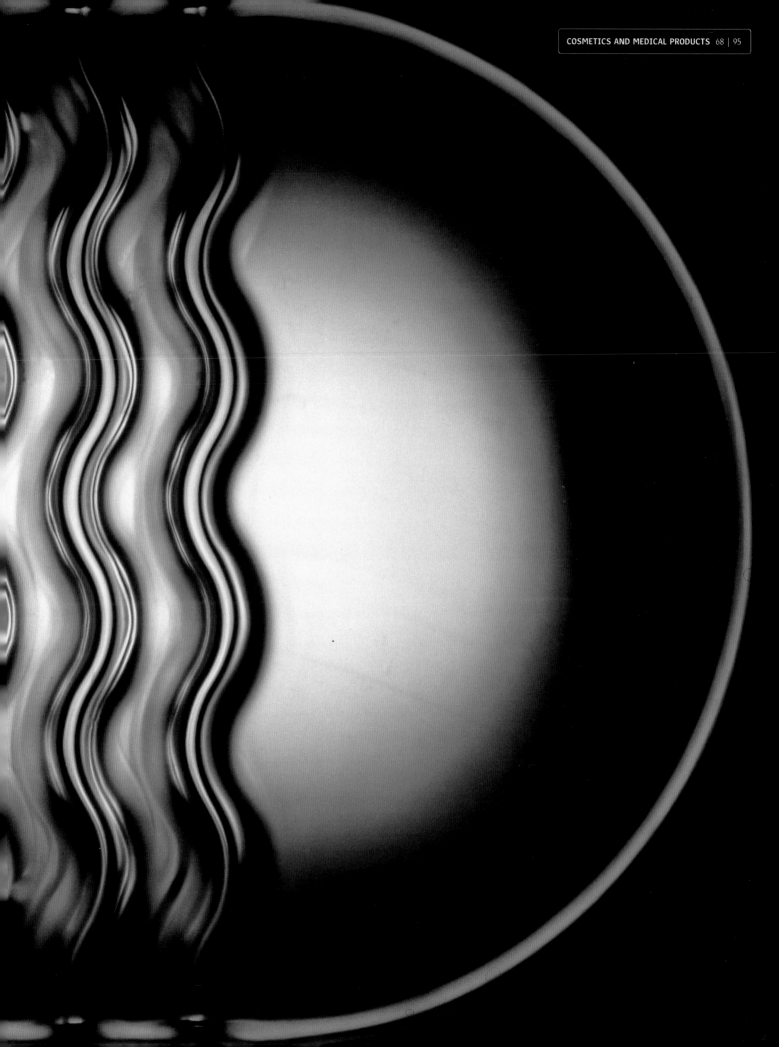

DESIGNER/ART DIRECTOR Kathy Miller
PROJECT DIRECTOR Siân Sutherland
DESIGN GROUP Miller Sutherland
CLIENT/MANUFACTURER Harris Oils Ltd

Following the successful launch of the Mio range, Miller Sutherland created this mini Escape Kit. Containing glass vials of specially blended concentrated bath oils, eau de cologne and peppermint gel, it is designed to help soothe away the stress of the day. The Mio branding carries through to this and two other products: a Love Kit, to encourage a romantic mood and a Sports Kit, to help one's body recover.

JOURNEY COLOGNE

DESIGNERS Mary Lewis,
Margaret Nolan, Peter Kay
ART DIRECTOR Mary Lewis
DESIGN GROUP Lewis Moberly
CLIENT/MANUFACTURER
Parfums Icardi Egan

Journey is a male fragrance positioned in the
mass market. It breaks new ground by moving
away from the macho overtones of the category,
towards a stronger expression of individuality
and sensitivity. It aims to present the consumer
with a voyage of discovery - an experience
reflected through the pace of the packaging.
Both bottle and outer carton offer layers of
intrigue and revelation. The frosted aquamarine
bottle is designed to feel slim in the hand and
cool to the touch, with a distinctive split profile
through bottle and cap and embossed detailing.
The identity is designed to be clear and simple.
The two-piece carton is unusual in a generally
bland category and is formed by two sections
which slide apart to reveal the fragrance bottle.
It has been carefully con- sidered to make it
a desirable container to keep.

DESIGNER/ART DIRECTOR Kathy Miller
PROJECT DIRECTOR Siân Sutherland
DESIGN GROUP Miller Sutherland
CLIENT/MANUFACTURER Harris Oils Ltd

Following the success of their premium range,
Harris Oils commissioned Miller Sutherland
to create a diffusion line of shower gels, eaux
de cologne, body lotions and bath oils in three
fragrances. This new range was to be aimed
at a broad spectrum of men and women who
appreciate quality bath and fragrance products.
Key to the mix was a new brand name, which
Miller Sutherland developed and allied to a
new logo. They added Superfresh, Supergentle
and Supercalm as descriptors, thus avoiding
any traditional aromatherapy language yet
still communicating the products' essential
benefits. The pack's graphics take the curve
from the Harris Oils premium range and diffuse
it in vivid colours which hint at the fragrance
blends. The complete range has tremendous
shelf-impact with its blocks of fresh, natural
colours, competing well with the handmade
papers and recycled browns of the competition.

RENAISSANCE MASSAGE OILS

DESIGNER/ART DIRECTOR/ILLUSTRATOR
Lydia Thornley
DESIGN GROUP
Lydia Thornley
CLIENT/MANUFACTURER
Renaissance Oils Ltd

The brief here was to package an entire range
of bath and massage oils in a way which would
express the quality of the products and their
positioning as a gift purchase. Individually,
the packaging had to convey the mood of each
oil. This was achieved by the use of colour
as well as a number of illustrations unique to
each product. A great deal of use and safety
information had to be included. This problem
has been overcome by using a tie-on label which
does not obscure the product, and, in fact, adds
to the overall impact of the package.

DESIGNERS Paul Davis, Russell Howorth
ART DIRECTOR Paul Davis
ILLUSTRATOR: Russell Howorth
DESIGN GROUP Agenda Design Associates
CLIENT/MANUFACTURER Bellview plc

Agenda Design Associates were commissioned
to create a distinctive new image and market
positioning for a range of 30 bath products.
The final design communicates the purity
of the various products' ingredients through
the use of colour and simplicity of form.
Similarly, the clear message achieved
through unadorned typography reinforces
the brand statement. The overall result
is a contemporary look in tune with today's
bathroom designs.

CONRAN

CONRAN
MANDARIN AND NEROLI BATH FOAM
BAIN MOUSSANT MANDARINE ET NEROLI

CONRAN

CONRAN BATH RANGE

DESIGNER/ART DIRECTOR Kathy Miller
PROJECT DIRECTOR Siân Sutherland
DESIGN GROUP Miller Sutherland
CLIENT/MANUFACTURER The Conran Shop

The Conran Shop commissioned Miller
Sutherland in 1995, briefing them to create
a new range of own-label bath products.
Taking responsibility for all aspects of
the packaging, Miller Sutherland sourced an
existing glass bottle from Italy and applied
the metal lashing tag and surface graphics.
They were also responsible for the
specification of the products' actual contents
and descriptors. In keeping with the general
Conran image, the bottle's shape is
accentuated while the stylishly simple
typography is kept to a minimum.

DESIGNER/ART Director Kathy Miller
PROJECT DIRECTOR Siân Sutherland
PHOTOGRAPHER Phil Jude
DESIGN GROUP Miller Sutherland
CLIENT/MANUFACTURER
Germaine de Capuccini

Miller Sutherland have been working with Germaine de Capuccini since 1993, re-designing all the company's products against a brief calling for brand identities which can enable the company to compete with their globally recognised rivals. Simplicity, elegance and attention to detail have been the touchstones of Miller Sutherland's success throughout this project. The bodycare range currently comprises products for use in bustcare, cellulite treatment and a handcream. The unusually honest approach of portraying a naked body on a pack is tempered by subtle washing of colour on the original black and white photographs, softening the imagery to create a look that is reminiscent of an oil painting.

DESIGNER/ART DIRECTOR Kathy Miller
PROJECT DIRECTOR Siân Sutherland
PHOTOGRAPHER DAVID Harrison
DESIGN GROUP Miller Sutherland
CLIENT/MANUFACTURER
Germaine de Capuccini

The Suncare range is one of the first lines
in Germaine de Capuccini's new luxury range
of products. The concept for this range is
the use of abstracted photography. The very
use of photography on skincare packaging
is a new and distinctive feature in the
international market. The colours of the pack
are sympathetic to sea/sand/sun imagery and
create a pack with very strong shelf-impact.

DESIGNERS Valerie Wickes, Charlie Thomas
ART DIRECTOR Valerie Wickes
DESIGN GROUP Din Graphics
CLIENT/MANUFACTURER French Connection

On 1st October 1995 French Connection
launched a fresh range of toiletries for
men and women. As an international
fashion label for men and women,
French Connection's clean, contemporary,
sexy image was the perfect inspiration
for developing a range of modern toiletries
that would appeal to all its customers.
The name, packaging and identity for
French Connection Bathroom was created
alongside the fresh citrus fragrance.
The range consists of eau du toilette,
bath oil, body creme, body lotion, bath
foam, shower gel, sea stones, a scented
candle and bath soap - and is not tested
on animals. The pure white boxes echo
pure white porcelain tiles, or fluffy
white bath robes, suggesting images
of freshness and cleanliness. Tactile,
chunky glass bottles and jars with
a contemporary and retro feel work with
the packaging to imply a fashionable
lifestyle without being dogmatic.
Although the range could not be any
simpler, with its black typography
and bright white boxes and labels,
it took an enormous effort to source
materials both white enough and
strong enough. The materials used
for the boxes, an exelda ivory board,
had not been used for box-making
before and had to undergo rigorous
tests before production.

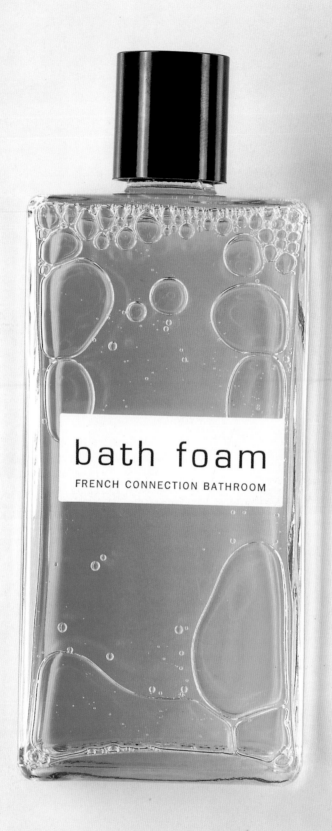

sea stones
FRENCH CONNECTION BATHROOM

PULBROOK & GOULD TOILETRIES RANGE

DESIGNERS Sarah Jane Hunter, Pene Parker
ART DIRECTOR Peter Windett
PHOTOGRAPHER Linda Burgess
DESIGN GROUP Peter Windett & Associates
CLIENT/MANUFACTURER Pulbrook & Gould

These toiletries called for a floral image
incorporated into their design, but with
a visual feel individual enough to reflect
the company's position as unique florists.
The design had also to appeal to selective
department stores both in the UK and USA.
The designers chose an unusual flower
pattern full of browns and purples set on
a deep green background in order to create
a rich, natural look that would still stand
out in a sector overcrowded with pastels.

SHE BEAUTY PRODUCTS RANGE

DESIGNER Antonia Hayward, Kevin Greene
ART DIRECTOR Tim Perkins, Peter Kay
DESIGN GROUP Design Bridge Ltd
CLIENT/MANUFACTURER Sara Lee

The original She range was launched by Sara Lee in Indonesia in the late 1980s, targeted at 20 year olds. After a relatively unsuccessful start, advertising was used to reposition the brand to appeal to a younger audience: firstly older teenagers and subsequently 13 to 17-year-olds. Whilst the advertising was extremely successful in raising the profile of the brand, the old pack design failed to support the new proposition. Design Bridge was therefore given a free rein to redesign both the graphic and physical packaging.

The main objectives of the brief were to appeal to the new target audience; to create a more distinctive physical pack, design one common bottle using shrink sleeving and rationalise the variants from five to three. The young, contemporary graphics communicate the nature of the body lotion, splash cologne, deodorant spray and perfumed talc featured in the range.

DESIGNER/ART DIRECTOR Kathy Miller
PROJECT DIRECTOR Siân Sutherland
DESIGN GROUP Miller Sutherland
CLIENT/MANUFACTURER John Lewis plc

The John Lewis Partnership's principal
philosophy is always to offer high quality
products which are good value for money,
and to convey this through their Jonelle
own-label packaging. The Jonelle range
of family toiletries had to reflect this
while still recognising that consumers
want good looking packs in their bathrooms.
The new range was extensive, so the design
solution had to work across several media.
Miller Sutherland were involved from the
very earliest stages of the project, from
the sourcing of structures right through
to the colours of the products themselves.
They recommended using simple structures
with innovative closures and pumps, and
that the products should be seen whenever
possible to give them an honest appeal.
Similarly, uncluttered typography is used
to convey the copy line 'Pure and Simple'
in a single band which gives the products
a distinctive look on shelves carrying more
brash brands. Since their launch in sales of
these products have increased by over 100%.

WAITROSE FOAM BATH

DESIGNER/ART DIRECTOR Kathy Miller
PROJECT DIRECTOR Siân Sutherland
ILLUSTRATOR Geoff Appleton
DESIGN GROUP Miller Sutherland
CLIENT/MANUFACTURER Waitrose

This brief from Waitrose was for the repackaging of their original bath foam range and the introduction of a complementary line of shower gels. The products are all good quality and have to compete mainly on price. The structures are all standardised, and the design had to work with limited colours. The final solution satisfies all the client's criteria by concentrating on an essential characteristic of all the products: bubbles. The classic typography conveys the quality of an essentially adult purchase and very clearly communicates the type of foam, creme or gel.

DESIGNER Sarah Roberts
ART DIRECTOR Gary Cooke
ILLUSTRATORS Mouseworks
DESIGN GROUP Horseman Cooke
CLIENT/MANUFACTURER Makro

A clean fresh approach was required
for the Aro Mint Mouthwash. Avoiding
the typographical styling of the major
brands, Horseman Cooke opted for
a strong image featuring a mint leaf
in the shape of a mouth, immediately
conveying the product's purpose.
The type is relatively restrained
to allow the branding to complement
the overall design. The strong concept
and minimal design are a good example
of effective but inexpensive packaging.

BOOTS PERFORMANCE

DESIGNER Harry Pearce
ART DIRECTORS Harry Pearce, Domenic Lippa
DESIGN GROUP Lippa Pearce Design Ltd
CLIENT/MANUFACTURER Boots The Chemist

To compete in an ever-growing market, Boots recently launched a range of specialist grooming products for men. The aim of the design was to project the products as state-of-the-art, using the physical characteristics of the products to enhance the designs. The understated concept uses the raw materials of the packaging to reinforce its positioning. The clean functional typography and strong masculine colour combination was vital in conveying the efficiency and added values of the range.

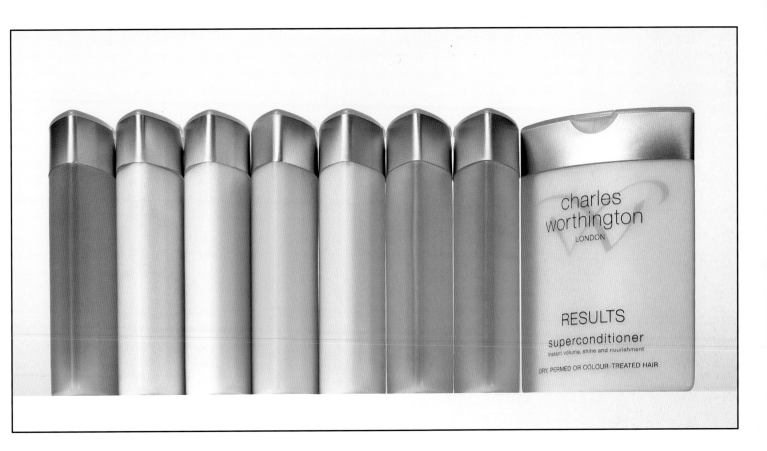

RESULTS HAIR CARE PRODUCTS

DESIGN GROUP Coley Porter Bell
CLIENT/MANUFACTURER Charles Worthington

In producing Results, Charles Worthington
wanted to create a new range of haircare
products which reflected his personality
as a hairdresser. The design was an integral
part of this. Despite the many hair products
on the market, the client felt that there was
still a need for those which combine the
latest in technology and performance with
the best in design and fragrance. Although
the range is aimed mainly at women, two
products are specifically for men, so the
designers had to ensure that the overall
presentation would appeal to both sexes.
The design takes its cue from other beauty
products rather than existing haircare ranges.
Results was created to look as good as other
fragrance and cosmetics products.
The bottles have been custom-tooled to form
sleek ellipses in natural frosted, recyclable
plastic. The shape is unique to the haircare
market, whilst being very ergonomic, and
the graphics endorse the sleek, clean feel.

DESIGNER Ian Stokes
ART DIRECTOR Robin Hall
DESIGN GROUP Davies Hall
CLIENT/MANUFACTURER Pitrok Ltd

Davies Hall were approached by Pitrok
to create a pack and brand identity for
this completely natural deodorant made
from natural mineral salts formed into
a long lasting crystal. Pitrok is
colourless and completely odourless.
The product needed to be positioned
as both a natural and environmentally
friendly product, with an appeal for both
sexes. The structural packaging evokes
the crystal formation and is designed
to contain the crystal without an inner
holder. The box is constructed out
of a minimum of 60% recycled board.
The use of minimal packaging and
uncoated recycled board helped to
reinforce the environmentally friendly
image of the deodorant. Simple graphics
and earthy colours were used to
differentiate it from the rest of the
deodorant market and to highlight its
naturalness.

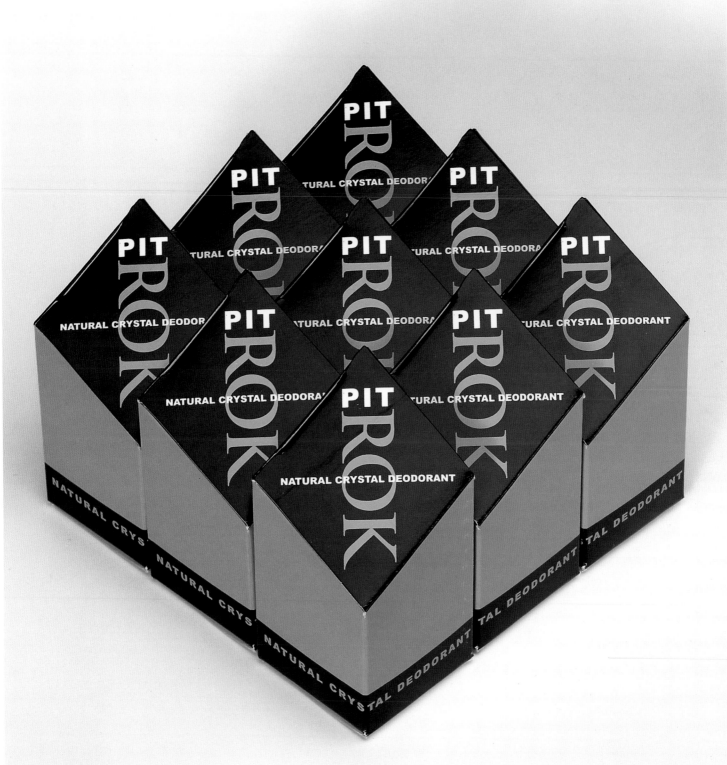

DESIGNER/ART DIRECTOR Glenn Tutssel
ILLUSTRATOR Colin Frewin
DESIGN GROUP Tutssels
CLIENT/MANUFACTURER Boots The Chemist

This handy pack of travel tissues was designed
to increase market share in tissues purchased
primarily for use on the move, on holiday or in
the car. Tutssels' aim was to reflect the usage
of these versatile tissues and play off the
many positive values associated with holidays:
fun, special occasions and travel. The solution
is a relevant design creatively using all
the graphic elements associated with travel.
Trains, planes, boats, and automobiles feature
throughout the packaging range.

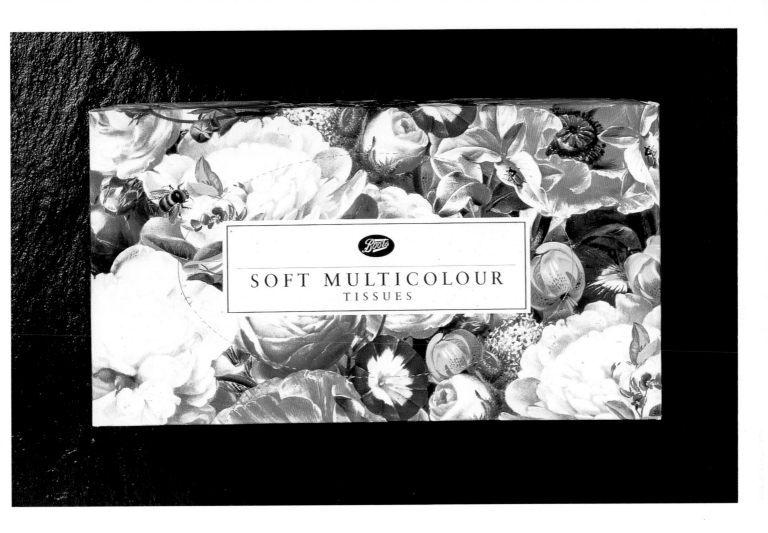

SOFT MULTICOLOUR
TISSUES

**BOOTS RECYCLED &
MULTI-COLOURED TISSUES**

DESIGNER David Pearman
ART DIRECTOR Glenn Tutssel
DESIGN GROUP Tutssels
CLIENT/MANUFACTURER Boots The Chemist

As part of the overall strategy to increase
market share in the tissue sector, Boots
asked Tutssels to redesign their existing
product range. Clear product benefits -
for example, multi-coloured and recycled
varieties - were to be highlighted.
Existing original flower paintings were
selected from archive material and retouched
to create the correct feel and colour value
of the tissues. The multicoloured product
features a brightly coloured range of flowers
while the recycled variety employs white
flowers with a green tint. The range identity
included toilet tissues, cosmetic and
decorated products.

NELSON'S CREAMS RANGE

DESIGNER/ART DIRECTOR Kathy Miller
PROJECT DIRECTOR Siân Sutherland
ILLUSTRATOR Geoff Appleton,
DESIGN GROUP Miller Sutherland
CLIENT/MANUFACTURER Waitrose

For Miller Sutherland, this was a challenging
brief from the leaders in homeopathy.
The redesign of the fourteen products in the
Nelson's range had to meet many criteria.
The products must look natural whilst
reassuring the consumer that they are just
as effective as the more brashly packaged
brands. Miller Sutherland's solution helps
the consumer understand exactly what each
product is used for by highlighting the
symptoms each treats in the centre of the pack.
The clean, fresh colours above the white base
help to reinforce the medicinal values while
simple illustrations depict the key ingredients
and communicate their natural origins.

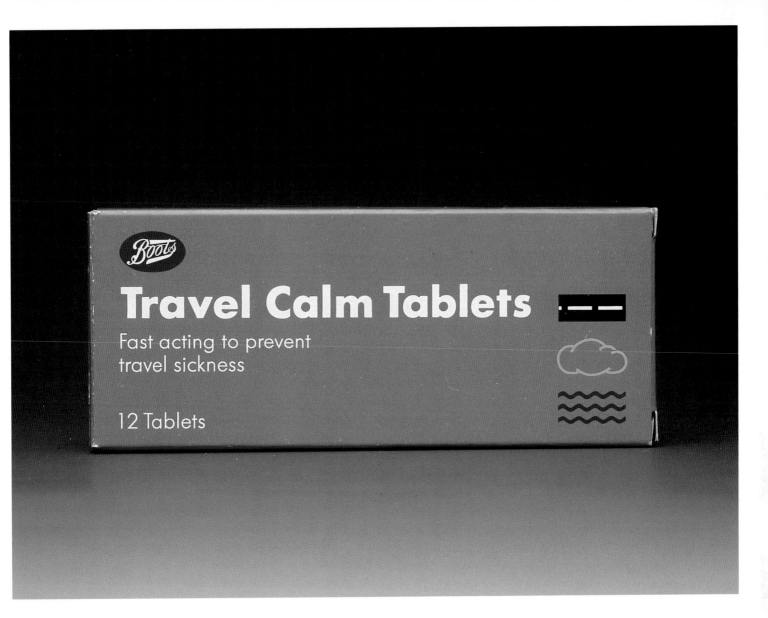

BOOTS TRAVEL CALM TABLETS

ART DIRECTORS Harry Pearce, Domenic Lippa
DESIGNERS Harry Pearce & Domenic Lippa
DESIGN GROUP Lippa Pearce Design Ltd
CLIENT/MANUFACTURER Boots The Chemist

As part of Boots' redesign of all their
healthcare packaging it was decided to
convey the efficacy of each product, as
well as Boots' core values. The graphics
had to be bold, simple and honest, hence
the adoption of the clean illustrative style.
The typography had already been developed
on earlier products and was continued
with this product. The packaging had to be
both informative and visually interesting
at the same time.

DESIGNER Harry Pearce
ART DIRECTORS Harry Pearce, Domenic Lippa
DESIGN GROUP Lippa Pearce Design Ltd
CLIENT/MANUFACTURER Boots The Chemist

New packaging concepts were required for
Boots' anti-insect bite products. The designs
needed to be strong and simple to quickly
convey the aims of the products. The designs
were to be a part of the redesign of Boots'
healthcare packaging and therefore had to
represent the confidence and strength for
which this brand is known.
The expressive use of yellow was common
in the original packs and was retained.
The road sign graphic device is used over
a line illustration of a mosquito.

DESIGNER Harry Pearce
ART DIRECTORS Harry Pearce, Domenic Lippa
ILLUSTRATOR Geoffrey Appleton
DESIGN GROUP Lippa Pearce Design Ltd
CLIENT/MANUFACTURER Boots The Chemist

Part of the problem in the redesign of the
Boots Vitamins range was how to build on
an already successful design which had
been diluted by the vast range of products
available. The designers' solution was to
retain the simple centred layout, knowing
that would be applicable to any shape of
product. The colour palette was
strengthened, making the colours brighter
to help on-shelf impact. The illustrations
were created in a more painterly way, thus
softening the redesign from its predecessor.
It was also felt that the illustrations could
work harder, so the designs reflect the
nature of the products through the
illustrations. In addition, a simple panelling
device is used to show the quantity and
strength of the pills and capsules. In all,
over 150 products were redesigned.

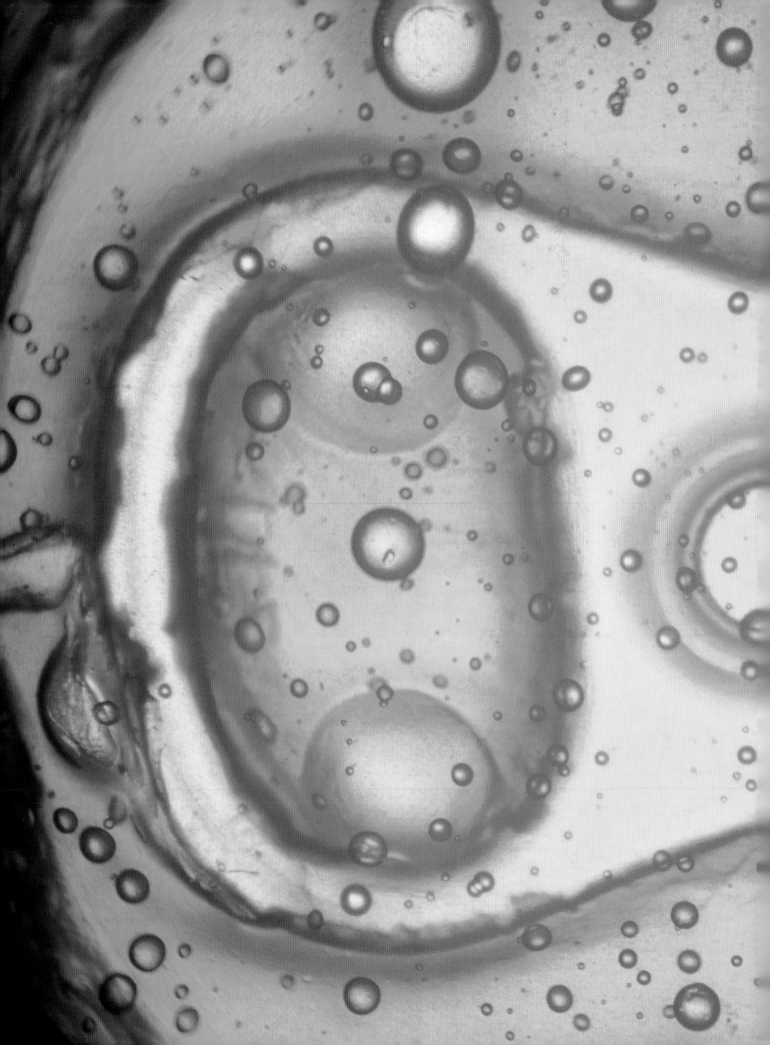

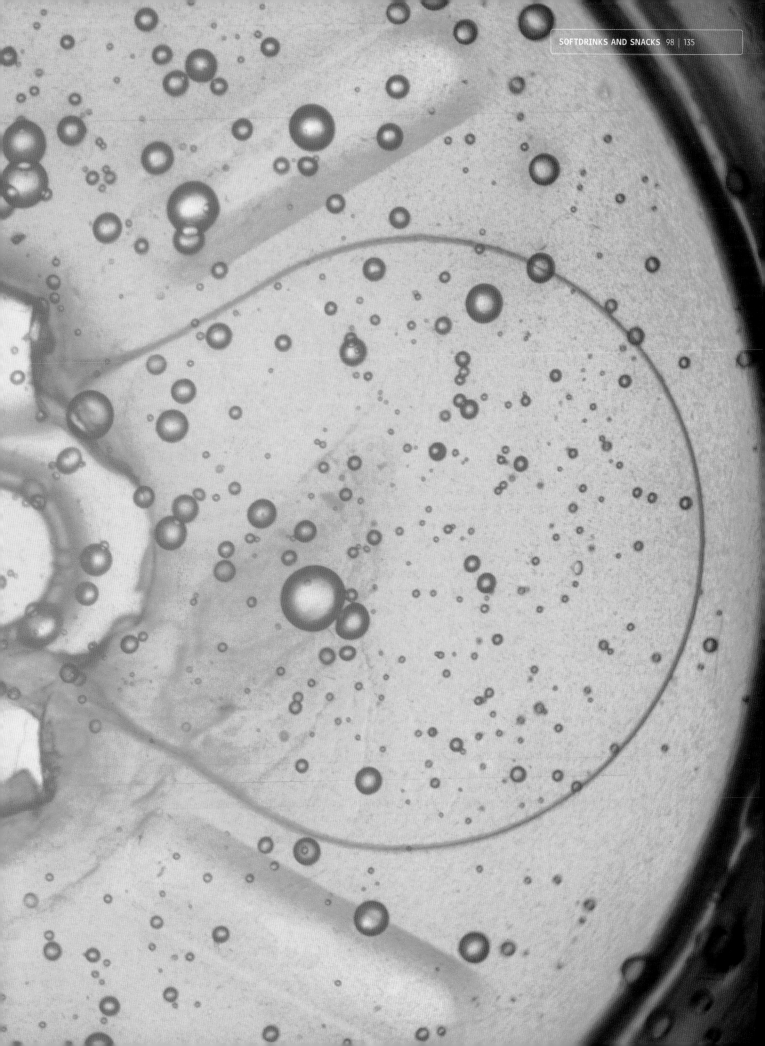

DESIGNER/ART DIRECTOR
Marcello Minale
DESIGN GROUP
Minale, Tattersfield & Partners Ltd.
CLIENT/MANUFACTURER
Osotspa

Osotspa commissioned design group Minale
Tattersfield to redesign their major energy
drink brand M150 for an international launch.
M150 is produced in Thailand and is mainly
sold there to 'hard hats' as an energy drink.
Osotspa wanted to broaden their market
area to include 'trendies' and young
energetic women. The new design will first
be introduced onto the existing bottles for
the Thai market but will be incorporated
onto cans for international introduction.
The graphic design retains the traditional
colours of red and yellow but adds silver
for a more techno appearance. The star
has been updated to project a more
futuristic feel.

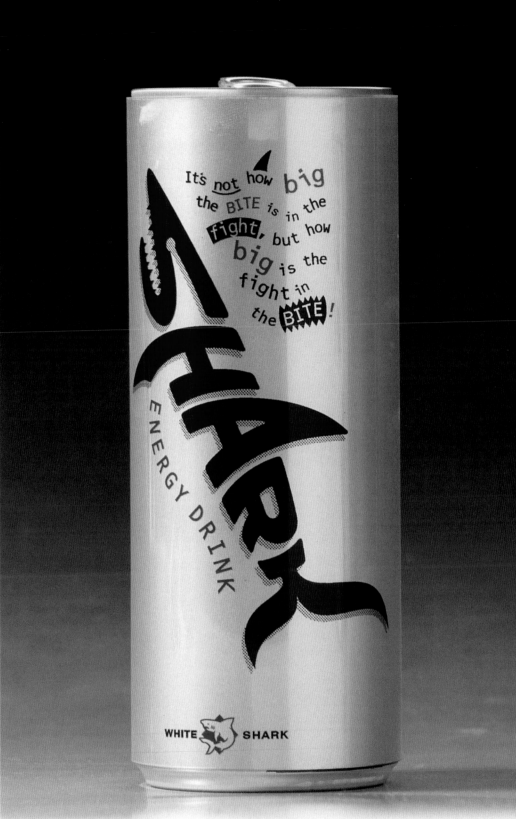

DESIGNER/ART DIRECTOR
Marcello Minale
DESIGN GROUP
Minale, Tattersfield & Partners Ltd.
CLIENT/MANUFACTURER
Osotspa

Shark is a high energy drink produced and sold in Thailand. The client, who wanted to reach the rest of the world, is competing against Red Bull, the major brand. Minale Tattersfield redesigned the product's image, making a radical change away from the old medicine-style bottle to a far more dynamic drink aimed primarily at the young and healthy adolescent. The new pack will be launched first in Thailand, China and Austria but will shortly be reaching other markets. The first packaging form will be basic cylindrical cans, to be followed by specially created bottles and other additions to the range.

DESIGNER Domenic Lippa
ART DIRECTORS Harry Pearce, Domenic Lippa
DESIGN GROUP Lippa Pearce Design Ltd
CLIENT/MANUFACTURER Sainsbury plc

The carbonated drinks market is complex
with many potential niche sectors. One
of the most active and growing is the youth
market. Sainsbury wanted to launch
a product in this sector. The product, unlike
most carbonates, had actual fruit flavours
added to it, thus creating a drink with the
dynamism of a traditional carbonate yet
with natural flavouring. To reflect this, the
designers used existing carbonate language,
such as italicised display typography within
a contemporary feel. Added to this are more
modern idiosyncratic values such as the
variants' subtitles - ace apple, cherry berry,
citrus cooler - displayed in the fun typeface
Dolores with a carbonated fruit illustration.
This was supported by the use of the can's
own silver substrate which again reinforced
the clear qualities of the product.

DESIGNERS
Bruce Duckworth, Janice L. Davison
ART DIRECTOR
Bruce Duckworth, David Turner
PHOTOGRAPHER Laurie Evans
DESIGN GROUP Turner Duckworth
CLIENT/MANUFACTURER
British Steel Tinplate

British Steel asked Turner Duckworth to
design a mailing piece to show the versatility
of their new shrink sleeve printing process
which is now available on steel softdrink
cans. This 'Pop Art' solution shows the
state-of-the-art process applied to pop cans.

SELTZER DRINKS

DESIGNER/ART DIRECTOR Sue Bicknell
ILLUSTRATOR Richard Duckett,
Cathy Ogilvie, Sue Bicknell
DESIGN GROUP Springett Associates
CLIENT/MANUFACTURER
The Seltzer Drinks Company Ltd

Seltzer is a naturally flavoured mineral water packaged in a clear can. When the client approached Springett Associates, the drink had been produced and canned in Iceland, using natural glacier water, but operations were moving to Wales, where the Seltzer partners had bought a factory. Their objective was to develop a new brand identity which would set the drink apart and increase its distribution. Apart from the clear can and the name, every element of the brand identity was open to reassessment. The design team believed that the core of Seltzer's identity should be irreverence - a special visual exuberance. The range of designs presented at this first stage reflected this in a variety of styles, from a grinning yellow monkey on the banana flavour to a huge floating cranberry printed on the back of the can and

seen through the clear liquid. The client's response was unique and intriguing. Instead of selecting one route to be developed, they wanted them all: a different design for each of their ten flavours and a new one for each subsequent flavour. Springett's task suddenly became one of creating a recognisable, ownable brand identity which was based on inconsistency. Redrawing the logo to make it more ownable, they placed it on a consistent branding band across the top of the can. This, together with the distinctive clear can, is the only element which remains static across the range. Consumers loved the new look and began to try the different flavours just to buy a different can. Listings soared, both in the UK and in Europe. Most significantly, the brand finally gained listings with two major UK multiples, so joining the major players.

ACQUA BRILLANTE

DESIGNER/ART DIRECTOR
Marcello Minale
DESIGN GROUP
Minale, Tattersfield & Partners Ltd
CLIENT/MANUFACTURER
Recoaro

Acqua Brillante is the leading brand of tonic water in Italy. Nevertheless, to reinforce its branding, a more powerful identity was sought. This design features an unmistakable, outsized water bubble supported by a shadow, brush stroke and new lettering which creates a unique identity. The blues and silvers incorporated into the clean, simple design immediately signal a refreshing drink.

DESIGNER/ART DIRECTOR
Gary Cooke
DESIGN GROUP
Horseman Cooke
CLIENT/MANUFACTURER
Makro

With the breakdown of the USSR, commercial enterprise and western design standards have become popular in Russia. The difficulty for any western designer who admires the strong graphic quality of Russian typography and imagery is avoiding such elements. Horseman Cooke had to make the Corona packaging look as if it had been imported from Manchester rather than Moscow. Using a very simple clean design based on the existing Corona logo style, they developed the design into its Russian namesake.

DESIGNER/ART DIRECTOR
Marcello Minale
DESIGN GROUP
Minale, Tattersfield & Partners Ltd
CLIENT/MANUFACTURER
San Pellegrino

Although San Pellegrino soft drinks are part of the Italian way of life, this brief called for an evolution of the Chino on-pack identity to bring it up to date. The colour coding remained the same, but the branding was made more dynamic and memorable by enclosing the key elements of the lettering and fruit in a single symbol. The typography was simplified to create a cleaner, more effective can.

DESIGNER/ART DIRECTOR
Marcello Minale
DESIGN GROUP
Minale, Tattersfield & Partners Ltd
CLIENT/MANUFACTURER
San Pellegrino

Although San Pellegrino soft drinks
are part of the Italian way of life,
this brief called for an evolution
of the Chino on-pack identity to bring
it up to date. The colour coding
remained the same, but the branding
was made more dynamic and
memorable by enclosing the key
elements of the lettering and fruit
in a single symbol. The typography
was simplified to create a cleaner,
more effective can.

DESIGNER
Tim Warren
ART DIRECTOR
Howard Milton
ILLUSTRATORS
Tim Warren, John Liddell
DESIGN GROUP
Smith & Milton Original
CLIENT/MANUFACTURER
SmithKline Beecham

Lucozade, the sparkling glucose drink marketed by SmithKline Beecham, has been popular since 1927. Traditionally seen as a convalescence and energy replacement drink, the brand has slowly shifted towards providing an energy boost in everyday life. It now has a strong sports association as well, particularly since the introduction of the isotonic range in the early 1990s. The radical redesign of the packaging began in late 1994 and can be summed up in one word: energy. The idea is that all the energy-giving power contained within the bottle is literally bursting to get out. The vertical logo which began life on a paper label was given greater power and impact when an alternative shrink-wrap label was used. The new, larger bottles have been strikingly redesigned to emphasise the various fruit flavours. The product's increased value for money is reflected in the fact that the larger bottles are sold at the same price as their smaller forbears, making them one of the most popular drinks on the market.

ACQUA BRILLANTE

DESIGNER/ART DIRECTOR
Marcello Minale
DESIGN GROUP
Minale, Tattersfield & Partners Ltd
CLIENT/MANUFACTURER
Recoaro

Acqua Brillante is the leading brand of tonic water in Italy. Nevertheless, to reinforce its branding, a more powerful identity was sought. This design features an unmistakable, outsized water bubble supported by a shadow, brush stroke and new lettering which creates a unique identity. The blues and silvers incorporated into the clean, simple design immediately signal a refreshing drink.

DESIGNERS Philip Carter, Teri Howes
ART DIRECTOR Philip Carter
ILLUSTRATOR Paul Slater
DESIGN GROUP Carter Wong & Partners
Client/Manufacturer AC Water Canada Inc.

Crystal Canadian is a branded mineral water bottled in Canada and specifically tailored for the British market. This packaging design, including the bottle shape, conveys the feelings of a fresh-tasting, pure, premium product and capitalises on its Canadian origins, which research showed had many positive connotations for a product of this nature. The maple leaf has valuable properties for Canada and Canadians worldwide. Believing that it would convey the product's origins quickly and effectively, Carter Wong obtained permission from the Canadian government to use the symbol as a feature of the packaging. The premium nature of the product is also enhanced by the colours used: a rich red for still mineral water and a deep blue for the sparkling variety. Each label is edged with silver while the typography introduces silver highlights. The bottle was chosen for its sophisticated shape; the maple leaf motif is reflected on the silver bottle cap. A small, elegant illustration on the label depicts a Canadian mountain scene, emphasising the purity of the location.

DESIGNER Karen Ellis
PHOTOGRAPHER Chris Harrison
DESIGN GROUP Elmwood Design
CLIENT/MANUFACTURER Orchid Drinks

The owners of the Monsoon brand had a clear proposition for this range of fruit-flavoured sparkling waters. Monsoon would deliver 'a rekindling of the taste buds'. The need to convey this exciting taste through the label design led to a solution very different from those favoured by sector rivals. Where others focus on the clarity of the product, Elmwood chose to bring out its fruity qualities, especially as the flavour combinations are rather unusual. The finished design features fruit pieces suspended in intensely coloured pools of water to reflect their ripe and refreshing flavours.

WAITROSE 10% JUICE CORDIALS

DESIGNER/ART DIRECTOR Darrell Ireland
PHOTOGRAPHER Patrice de Villiers
DESIGN GROUP The Foundry Design Consultants Ltd
CLIENT/MANUFACTURER Waitrose

The designer was interested in the close-quarter
details of the fruits used in Waitrose's juices.
When each image was placed centrally in its
main panel, it was possible to read what the
product was from a distance, without having to
get close enough to read the name of the product.
Close to the product the image became more
diffused and relied on the name tag ribbon device
to give an overall identity and cohesion to the
product names. Patrice de Villiers photographed
all the fruit with great care and attention to
detail, even colour coding each background and
painting them herself. Finally all the products
were shot on 35mm to get the maximum grain
effect possible. The result is a striking image
based on a strong concept.

DESIGNERS Darrell Ireland, Melanie Ryan
ART DIRECTOR Darrell Ireland
ILLUSTRATOR George Marshall
DESIGN GROUP The Foundry
Design Consultants Ltd
CLIENT/MANUFACTURER Waitrose

Waitrose used to sell their juices in PET bottles, but wanted to move out over to Tetra packs with nozzles to increase efficiency and the product shelf-life. The brief was to cover these details and ensure that the three main product types, the lemonade being a summer-only product, were all related through agreed graphic devices. The Foundry chose illustrator George Marshall for his consummate painting skill and impressionistic style, bringing to mind images of Gauguin and Cézanne. To offset these lively impressions, the designers applied a simple typographic statement, clearly naming and colour-coding the product. Waitrose are now selling more than double the annual amount sold in PET.

SAN PELLEGRINO FOUR-PACK CASES

DESIGNER/ART DIRECTOR Marcello Minale
DESIGN GROUP Minale, Tattersfield & Partners Ltd
CLIENT/MANUFACTURER San Pellegrino

Italian soft drinks giant San Pellegrino
launched the new packaging for two of
their major brands - Chino and Aranciata
- with design by Minale, Tattersfield
& Partners Ltd. Aranciata, the number
one orange drink in Italy, ahead of
competitors Orangina and Fanta, has
incorporated the corporate influence
of the famous San Pellegrino star in
the form of bubbles floating up the front
of the pack and as the stalk tummy-button
of the orange.
Chino is a drink particularly favoured by
Italians. It looks like cola but tastes like
a mixture of cola and orangeade. There
are over one-hundred chino-style drinks on
the market in Italy, but San Pellegrino
are so confident their product will become
the leader that they called it Chino 1.

DESIGNER/ART DIRECTOR Antonia Eckersley
DESIGN GROUP Springett Associates
CLIENT/MANUFACTURER Dairy Crest

Dairy Crest was gathering its assets in preparation for launch as a public company. As a part of this exercise, the company wanted to add a strong fresh milkshake brand to its portfolio. They appointed Springett Associates to help them invent, design and develop this brand in every aspect from name to packaging shape to distinctive, powerful graphics.

The result was brand-leading Frijj. The designers emphasised the fresh nature and immediacy of the milk drink by building in an element of elasticity and change to the brand identity. They selected a shrink-wrapped labelling process which not only allowed the branding to extend to the whole pack, but also allowed the label to be changed quickly and easily.

To boost sales in winter - a low period for cold drinks - a limited edition range of labels for Halloween was easily produced, as were later versions for Easter and Christmas. Without advertising or other promotion, Frijj quickly rocketed to become a market leader, winning Springett Associates a coveted DBA Design Effectiveness award.

KING OSCAR FISH PRODUCTS

DESIGNER Brian Webb,
Lynn Trickett, Andrew Thomas
ART DIRECTOR Brian Webb, Lynn Trickett
ILLUSTRATOR John Lawrence
DESIGN GROUP Trickett & Webb Ltd
CLIENT/MANUFACTURER King Oscar Foods

The sardine canning industry grew up in
Norway at the end of the last century
when sardines exported from Norway were
traditionally given private labels by each
importer. This caused confusion over the years
with several brand names and label designs
being used for the same product in the USA.
The King Oscar Company, one of Norway's
oldest sardine exporters, asked Trickett &
Webb to rationalise its sardine packaging
with the intention of building a brand
recognisable throughout the world. Obvious
traditional images were retained, including
the King Oscar portrait, crown and ribbons.
Packaging for the new fish products also
uses the existing design elements but with
a seascape background illustrating the origins
of the product. Although product descriptions
are translated into many languages for new
markets which include South America and the
Far East, the visual references have helped
consumers understand the new range.

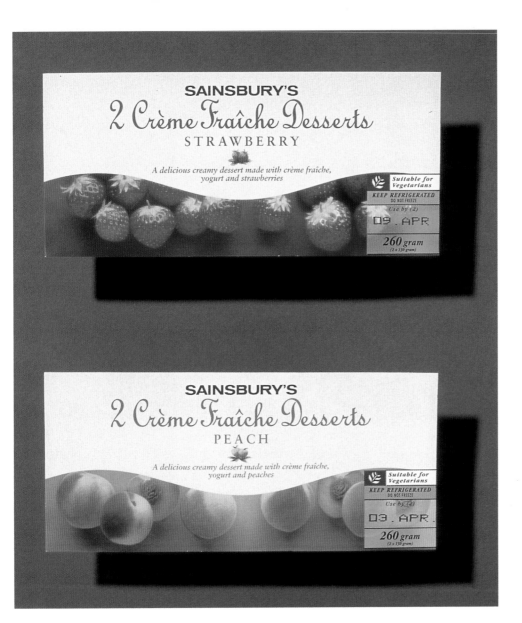

SAINSBURY CREME FRAÎCHE

DESIGNER Michael Davies
ART DIRECTORS Harry Pearce, Domenic Lippa
PHOTOGRAPHER Richard Foster
DESIGN GROUP Lippa Pearce Design Ltd
CLIENT/MANUFACTURER Sainsbury

When asked to design a new range of creme fraîche packaging for Sainsbury, the designers realised that if the range was to be successful the design solution should reflect the premium quality of the product as well as differentiating it from competitive products. Lippa Pearce achieved this through a strong curving branding device which realised two objectives: it acted as a natural display area for the basic product information, and it reinforced the creamy quality of the product. This was combined with a rich photograph of the natural ingredients. The use of Linoscript then added a degree of quality to the layout.

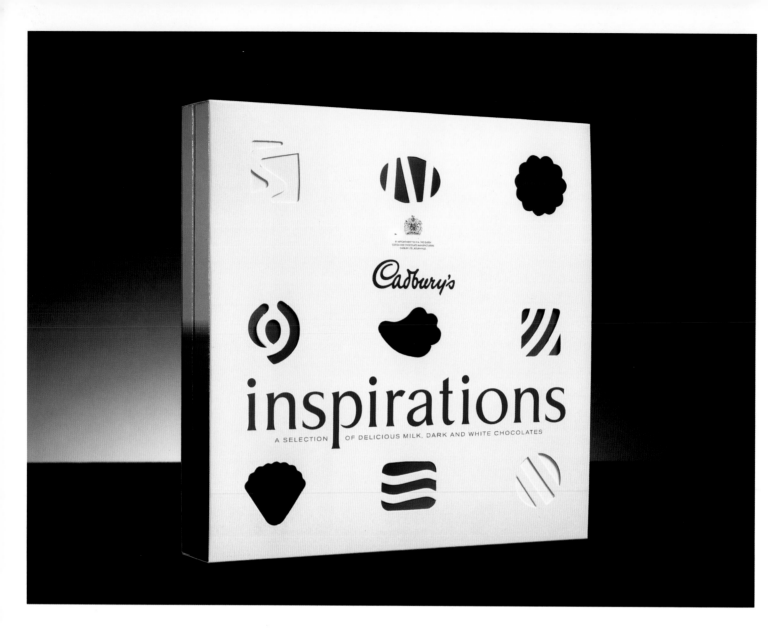

INSPIRATIONS CHOCOLATES

DESIGN GROUP Coley Porter Bell
CLIENT/MANUFACTURER Cadbury Ltd

Originally launched in 1989, Inspirations'
mix of chocolates is popular with consumers.
However, research found that its packaging
design - four stacked drawers of chocolates
contained in a box - did not build on the
value of the product and failed to reflect
'chocolateness' at all.
Cadbury's decided to redesign it to enable it
to compete successfully in the sophisticated
value sector of the boxed chocolates market,
dominated by Fererro Rocher. Brands in this
sector have a variety of uses, from intimate
gifts to self-indulgent presents, and are seen
as suitable thank you and dinner party gifts.
The new design retains the idea of an intriguing
box, gradually revealing the chocolates inside,
but in a simpler, one-layer form. The inner box,
contained in a sleeve, is a dark chocolate
colour fading to white, emphasising the three

different types of chocolate contained in the
box. Cut-outs in the top of the sleeve indicate
the chocolate shapes and focus on the intricacy
of the product itself.

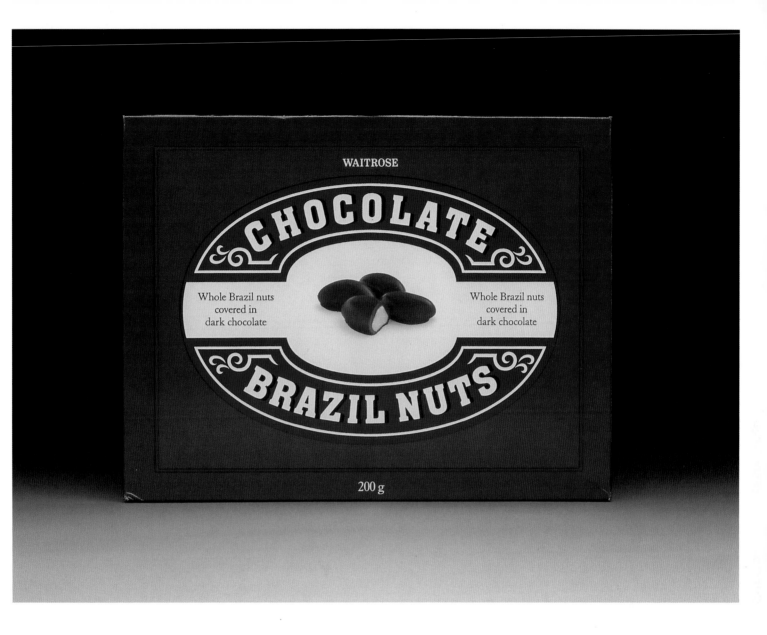

WAITROSE CHOCOLATE BRAZIL NUTS

DESIGNER Domenic Lippa
ART DIRECTOR Harry Pearce, Domenic Lippa
DESIGN GROUP Lippa Pearce Design Ltd
CLIENT/MANUFACTURER Waitrose

As a retailer, Waitrose have a history of
individual packaging design which in itself
is a reflection of their character.
The quality of their products is high and
this is reflected in their packaging design.
To enable the designers to maintain this
quality, great care and detail was required.
In the case of these premium chocolates,
the solution was to use typography and colour
to convey the indulgent connotations of the
chocolates. The hand-drawn lettering captures
the character of the confectionery.
The border device, simple line illustration
of the chocolate and colour scheme based
on chocolate hues, has in itself a strong
shelf-impact.

BAHLSEN FAMILY BISCUITS

DESIGNER/ART DIRECTOR Mary Lewis
PHOTOGRAPHER Robin Broadbent
DESIGN GROUP Lewis Moberly
CLIENT/MANUFACTURER Bahlsen Keksfabrik KG

Bahlsen is the leading German premium
biscuit brand. As the name suggests, this
is a range to be enjoyed by all the family -
there is something in this assortment for
everyone. The concept aims to project this.
Each variety is carefully identified and
they come together to form a biscuit family.
When the packs are positioned alongside
each other on the shelf, they form a long
chain of figures holding hands, creating
a powerful in-store display.

DESIGNER Ian Prewett
ART DIRECTOR Brian Delaney
PHOTOGRAPHER Carol Sharp
DESIGN GROUP Delaney Design Consultants
CLIENT/MANUFACTURER Waitrose Ltd

Waitrose commissioned Delaney Design
Consultants to produce designs for their
Orange and Ginger Plain Chocolate Crunch
biscuit range. This simple uncluttered
design features the product in an atmospheric photographic style emphasising
the indulgent quality of the richly flavoured
plain chocolate biscuits. The background
colour and texture reflect the flavour of
each pack.

FORTNUM AND MASON BISCUIT RANGE

DESIGNERS Sarah Jane Hunter, Pene Parker
ART DIRECTOR Peter Windett
ILLUSTRATOR Tom King
DESIGN GROUP Peter Windett & Associates
CLIENT/MANUFACTURER Fortnum & Mason

This design, for Fortnum and Mason Biscuits
for both the domestic and export markets,
needed to have an English feel, yet the image
must be one that people could relate to on
an international level. The packaging includes
individual and gift cartons which feature
images drawn from the famous Piccadilly
facade. The decorative though not overcrowded
design is what was needed for this up-market
biscuit.

WHITTARD OF CHELSEA BISCUIT BOXES

DESIGNER Jan Atkins
ART DIRECTOR Alan Colville
ILLUSTRATOR Alison Jay
DESIGN GROUP Ian Logan Design Company
CLIENT/MANUFACTURER Whittard of Chelsea

Whittard of Chelsea is a well established tea
and coffee company with a dynamic
management team and upwards of 80 stores
in the UK. Ian Logan Design have created more
than 80 tea and coffee packs for them and were
asked to extend this successful record into
labelling for other product lines. The designers
took an English theme for the biscuits, with
strong, original artwork which evokes
traditional values and subjects (including rural
scenes such as the country fair and harvest)
and give an impression of the highest quality.
The crackle finish is a tongue-in-cheek 'ageing',
linking the illustrations to antique oil
paintings. By using modern, entertaining
illustrative styles these traditional subjects
are transformed into something contemporary
and relevant. The biscuit tins fit very happily
into today's interiors and are attractive
enough in themselves to be seen as gift items.

DESIGNER/ART DIRECTOR Martyn Hayes
ILLUSTRATOR John Richardson
DESIGN GROUP Elmwood Design
CLIENT/MANUFACTURER
Kraft Jacob Suchard

The brief here was to produce a pack
of distinction and old worldliness,
with a particular appeal to adults.
The tin container works on a number
of levels. Fundamentally it keeps
the product fresher and it's easier
and more attractive to pass around.
Symbolically the tin appears unusual,
yet it has an aura of solidity and
is old-fashioned. The paper liner is
in tune with the overall feeling of
the package. Finally, the graphics
and typography are traditional; the
colours of white and green convey
mint values, while red communicates
extra-strong taste. To achieve the
desired elements of quirkiness and
uniqueness the designers chose
silver for the colour of the tin.

...iously

...RONG MINTS

...spite their diminutive nature,
...e should not underestimate the
...ity of these small peppermints to
...resh the palate.

DESIGNER
Marc Wittenberg
ART DIRECTOR
David Wombwell
DESIGN GROUP
Ziggurat
CLIENT/MANUFACTURER
KP Skips Corn Snacks

Skips is the favourite snack amongst
eight to twelve year old children in the
UK. The object of this redesign was to
maximise the brand's communication
with this group by strengthening its
visual identity on the pack. The way the
product eats is key to the new look: kids
enjoy the way it fizzles and melts in their
mouths, bending and trans- forming in
a unique and special eating experience.
The previous pack and branding did little
to suggest this. The use of fun, bending
lettering and borders directly expresses
the way kids experience the product
melting in their mouths.
The whole presentation has been made
more fluid and soft, so the brand looks
the way the snack tastes and feels.
To achieve the desired visual effect of
energy and personality, Ziggurat created
every part of the design by hand, crafting
the design in the traditional way on the
drawing board before transposing into
the digital artwork environment. Using the
structural possibilities of reprographics,
the designers have achieved a great
diversity and saturation of tone from
only five colours.

DESIGNERS
Darrell Ireland, Melanie Ryan
ART DIRECTOR
Darrell Ireland
ILLUSTRATOR
Jeremy Sancha
DESIGN GROUP
The Foundry Design Consultants Ltd
CLIENT/MANUFACTURER
Waitrose

The challenge with snack packaging
is to make a quality product stand
out in a market saturated with glaring
graphics. Integrity and value have
to be conveyed, as well as a sense
of tradition. The Foundry's solution
to the challenge was to use a touch
of illustrative sorcery, an idea that
proved to sell. Since the introduction
of this own brand, sales have increased
enormously while sales of the brand
leader have remained the same.
Waitrose, having established a foothold
in this area, plan to expand the range
in the near future.

WAITROSE BELGIAN CHOCOLATE SEASHELLS

DESIGNER/ART DIRECTOR Kathy Miller
PROJECT DIRECTOR Siân Sutherland
ILLUSTRATOR Geoff Appleton
DESIGN GROUP Miller Sutherland
CLIENT/MANUFACTURER Waitrose Food Stores

Miller Sutherland were asked to design the
packaging for Waitrose Belgian Chocolate
Seashells, a product which, with its slight
eccentricity, needed to be shown on the pack.
The design solution neatly avoids the use
of a cheap-looking acetate window by using
illustrations all over the pack. The creation
of a crest from the varying seashells has
a tongue-in-cheek wit about it that combines
with the classic typography and rich brown /
black background to give a real quality
impression. The front shells are embossed
to add dimension and judicious use of gold
blocking helps to build on its premium look.

PICNIC CHOCOLATE BAR

DESIGNER Louise Wardle
ART DIRECTOR Ian Ritchie
DESIGN GROUP Jones Knowles Ritchie
CLIENT/MANUFACTURER Cadbury Ltd

Picnic bars were first introduced in 1959
and are well established in their sector.
However, the brand had achieved relatively
low impact and, because of its cream
packaging, was sometimes misunderstood
as a cereal bar. Moving right away from
any cereal associations, the new packaging
places Picnic firmly alongside its mainstream
chocolate competitors. With its rich colours
and clean logotype it now has much more
impact as an impulse purchase fighting for
market share in a crowded sector.

RICHLY CARAMELISED NUT RANGE

DESIGNER Victor Liew
ART DIRECTOR Judi Green
ILLUSTRATOR Andrew Riley
DESIGN GROUP The Green House
CLIENT/MANUFACTURER Richly Ltd

Richly supply expensive gourmet nuts
and confectionery to the premium end
of the market in the UK and Germany.
With the products currently packaged
in clear plastic boxes, Richly were under
pressure from retailers to repackage
their products in jars, in order to extend
their shelf life and freshness.
This created conflict between the quality
aspects, premium price and convenience
of the product. The Green House were
briefed to create a unique brand identity
and label design for a range of six
caramelised nuts with the aim of moving
the brand into a more mainstream market,
whilst still retaining a premium feel and
a modern contemporary look.

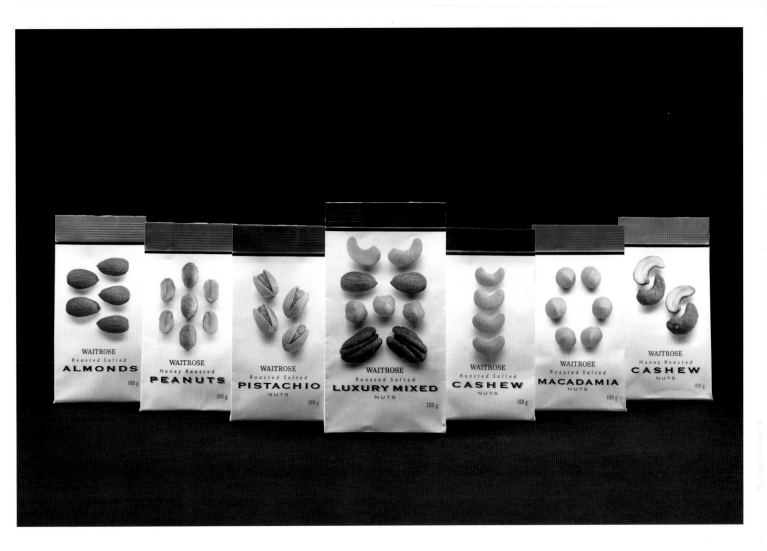

WAITROSE LUXURY NUTS

DESIGNER/ART DIRECTOR Kathy Miller
PROJECT DIRECTOR Siân Sutherland
PHOTOGRAPHER David Gill
DESIGN GROUP Miller Sutherland
CLIENT/MANUFACTURER Waitrose Food Stores

Waitrose's brief to Miller Sutherland was simple: to create new packaging for a range of nuts which would have to compete with major brands in the market. The other main consideration was that the nuts should be visible in their packs as some proposed varieties would be unfamiliar to some customers. Miller Sutherland recommended the introduction of foil block-bottomed bags to increase the overall packaging quality. The graphic symmetry of the nuts and the use of photography help to convey the premium aspects of the range and give the packs exceptional standout.

DESIGN GROUP Newell and Sorrell Ltd
ILLUSTRATOR Tania Hurt-Newton
CLIENT/MANUFACTURER Boots The Chemist

Boots Animal Shaped Biscuits are part of
a range of Boots' foods for the toddler age
group. The packs are designed to be fun
and appeal to toddlers while at the same
time have a reassuring image for parents
who want to give their children the best.
The lively illustrations on the pack are
reflected in the shapes of the biscuits
themselves, and the pack has been designed
to have play value after its original use.

DESIGNERS Karen Welman, Nicola Waller
ART DIRECTOR Karen Welman
ILLUSTRATORS Simon Critchley, Steve Pearce
DESIGN GROUP Pearlfisher International
Design Partnership
CLIENT/MANUFACTURER Pearlfisher Design

How often does a design company specialising
in brands actually demonstrate it by launching
its own? Pearlfisher became their own client
and turned their conceptualising skills to
the creation of a premium tea and biscuit set
based on the Mad-Hatter's tea party. Each pack
consists of a variety of four specially selected
teas and biscuits contained within a unique box
that folds outwards when the lid is removed.
All aspects of concept creation, from sourcing,
printing, packaging, and shipping to selling,
brought Pearlfisher into first-hand contact with
many aspects of brand-building which are often
unappreciated by design consultancies. They have
high hopes for their brand's continued success.

DESIGNER Simon Thorneycroft
DESIGN DIRECTOR Andrew King
CREATIVE DIRECTOR Richard Ford
DESIGN GROUP Landor Associates
CLIENT/MANUFACTURER Nestle Lyons Maid

Launched in 1963, Fab is one of the most established brands in the UK ice cream market. For most of its life, the brand has been positioned as an ice lolly for girls. Following research which indicated Fab appealed equally to boys and girls, the brand was repositioned to target both sexes. It was felt that the packaging for Fab needed to be redesigned to reflect more accurately the brand's positioning and personality. The repositioning of Fab was driven initially by advertising, which had led to a significant increase in sales. The new positioning - 'There's more to Fab than your average ice lolly' - reflected the product's distinctive characteristics (strawberry, vanilla, chocolate and hundreds and thousands) and the brand's fun, quirky personality.

The new design needed to reflect the unique nature of the product and communicate the brand personality whilst remaining faithful to the core equities which consumers associate with the brand. Landor's solution is a witty and involving interpretation of the key product characteristics and reflects the brand personality perfectly.
It appeals to children and adults alike, and has an energy designed to make it stand out on the shelf. The designers retained the three stages of the lolly - strawberry, vanilla, and hundreds and thousands - and redrew the Fab identity to make it more youthful and friendly. They also introduced an explosive feel and other fun elements such as flying strawberries, lips, hands and faces to communicate the taste experience.

DESIGN DIRECTOR Andrew King
CREATIVE DIRECTOR Richard Ford
DESIGN GROUP Landor Associates
CLIENT/MANUFACTURER
Walkers Snack Food Ltd

Launched in 1967, Doritos is a brand leader in the USA. Believing the brand to have global potential, the client asked Landor to create a visual identity which would work at both local and international levels. Landor used their international network of offices to analyse the various requirements of differing markets and recommended a design strategy which called for a powerful brand icon which could be used in both on-pack and off-pack situations. The creative solution is a dynamic chip device which embodies the essential fun and irreverence of the Doritos brand; the triangular product 'window' reinforces this imagery. Each package is visually split so that the lower half carries the flavour colour while the use of a consistent brand colour unifies the range. The new design has rejuvenated the increasingly niche corn snack category and has been regarded by many as the most successful salty snack launch ever.

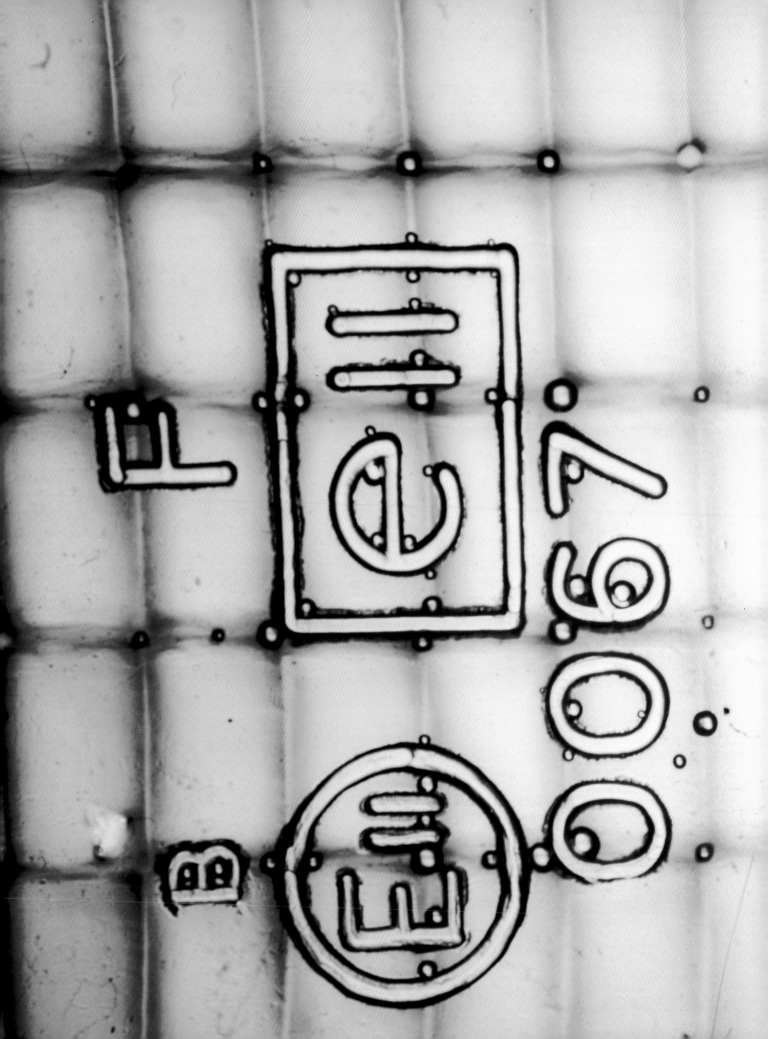

DESIGNERS Don Williams,
Richard Evans, Steve Kelsey
CREATIVE DIRECTOR
Don Williams, Steve Kelsey
DESIGN ENGINEER Jed O'Brien
DESIGN GROUP P. I. Design International
CLIENT/MANUFACTURER Shell International

This design for a new car care range from
Shell Chemical Europe shows the integration
of structure and graphics: the smooth, elegant
lines of the bottle work in sympathy with
the arched labels. The black background of the
labels contrasts well with the silvery metallic
plastic containers. The design also unifies
a family of more than 30 products into four
categories, available in four pack sizes.
The overall effect is one of simplicity and
understatement.

JET MAX MOTOR OIL

DESIGNER/ART DIRECTOR Steve Kelsey
DESIGN GROUP P. I. Design International
CLIENT/MANUFACTURER Conoco Ltd

Conoco's market research showed that its Jet brand was perceived as being of a lower quality and performance than major brands such as Castrol, despite the fact that its specification is comparable. The designers' brief was to create a new identity for the product by redesigning both the structure of the pack and its surface graphics. The structural solution focuses on offering consumers a pack with a unique easy-pour closure. The purpose here is to appeal to motorists who dislike handling motor oil. The consumer friendly approach was a success; supported only by trade press advertising, sales in the first year after the launch rose by 33%.

DESIGNER Harry Pearce
ART DIRECTORS Harry Pearce, Domenic Lippa
COPYWRITER Giles Calver
PHOTOGRAPHER Richard Foster
DESIGN GROUP Lippa Pearce Design Ltd
CLIENT/MANUFACTURER Halfords

As part of the total redesign of all their own-brand packaging, Halfords wanted to re-establish confidence within the brand as well as increase general sales. This was achieved by developing a concept strongly based on information. All relevant copy was laid out in a very systemised way, highlighting the unique benefits of the products. The use of strong black and white photography reinforced the positioning and usage of the products. In addition, lifestyle images helped reflect the type of environment the product would be used in. The range was divided into premium and standard products by the green and terracotta palettes.

DESIGNER Harry Pearce
ART DIRECTORS Harry Pearce, Domenic Lippa
COPYWRITER Giles Calver
PHOTOGRAPHER Richard Foster
DESIGN GROUP Lippa Pearce Design Ltd
CLIENT/MANUFACTURER Halfords

Lippa Pearce were asked to redesign all
Halfords' aerials and accessory products
as part of the total re-evaluation of
the Halfords brand. The accessories range
had to complement the core range but
at the same time have maximum individual
on-shelf impact. The designers chose
a neutral background of grey to help
project the actual products.
A strong, informative illustration was
then incorporated into the front face,
showing how the product worked.

ASSET CAR PARTS

DESIGNER/ILLUSTRATOR Paul Cilia La Corte
ART DIRECTOR John Blackburn
DESIGN GROUP Blackburn's Ltd
CLIENT/MANUFACTURER
Automotive Distributors Ltd

Automotive Distributors Limited, the UK's
leading importer of Japanese car components,
needed an identity for a new value-led range
of products.
Blackburn's named the brand Asset and created
a design which uses the language of the market
to signpost each product's proposition. The red
triangle echoes the 'A' of Asset and simple
symbols communicate each type of component.
In an increasingly commodity-driven sector,
Asset has been developed as a distinctive
brand, fully in tune with its product category.

MAISTO SUPERCAR COLLECTION

DESIGNER/ART DIRECTOR Lynn McKenna
ILLUSTRATOR Martin Sexton
DESIGN GROUP Greenwich Design Associates
CLIENT/MANUFACTURER Shell UK Ltd

The only constraint in this brief was the use
of a standard box construction to create
a strong, simple identity across a range of
sportscar packaging to be displayed in Shell
Service Stations nationwide. The design had
to reflect the quality and value associated
with this major retailer.
Through Futura text and colours derived from
Shell's new Retail Visual Identity Colour
Palette, graphics were kept to a minimum,
complementing the product itself. Movement
and racing connotations were created by the
use of a chequered flag on the left hand side,
fading to yellow on the right.

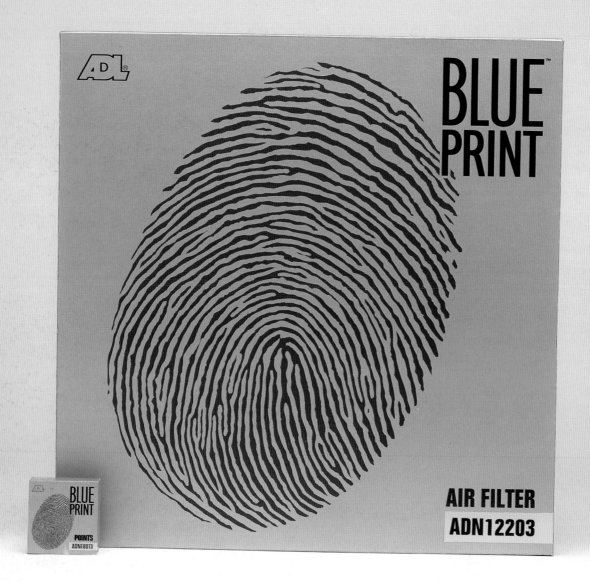

BLUE PRINT COMPONENTS

DESIGNER Belinda Duggan
ART DIRECTOR John Blackburn
ILLUSTRATOR Matt Thompson
DESIGN GROUP Blackburn's Ltd
CLIENT/MANUFACTURER
Automotive Distributors Ltd

Automotive Distributors Limited wanted their high quality components to make a clear statement about specialisation in a market well-known for notoriously bland packaging that makes most products look like commodities. Blackburn's created the name Blue Print to reflect the products' premium status and the highly specialised nature of their manufacturing tolerances. The new design, with its distinctive blue finger print, is not only individual but recognisable and raises the brand far above the commodity crowd. The marque is also internationally understood for easy interpretation that doesn't rely on words alone.

DESIGNER/ART DIRECTOR Brian Delaney
Photographer Colin T. Gifford
Design Group Delaney Design Consultants
Client/Manufacturer Royal Mail Design Division

Royal Mail commissioned Delaney Design
Consultants to design the Age of Steam stamps
and presentation pack. The group chose to focus
on the period most people could relate to - the
last decade of steam - and to use photographic
images. Photographer Colin Gifford's evocative
and sensitive approach to the subject conveyed
exactly the importance of the setting and also
the atmosphere of the railways chosen.
The presentation pack concentrates on the many
ways the steam engine affected everyday life -
from toy trains and holiday excursions through
to everyday commuting.

ASHIMA FISHING LINE

DESIGNER Bruce Duckworth
ART DIRECTOR
Bruce Duckworth, David Turner
DESIGN GROUP Turner Duckworth
CLIENT/MANUFACTURER
Ashima Fishhook Company

In creating the brand identity and packaging for The Ashima Fish Hook Company, Turner Duckworth wanted to develop a high impact identity communicating the exceptionally efficient nature of the equipment. Bold, simple graphics and colour coding were used on specialised film to communicate clinical efficiency in a way which allows the product, packaging, format and graphics to work in concert.

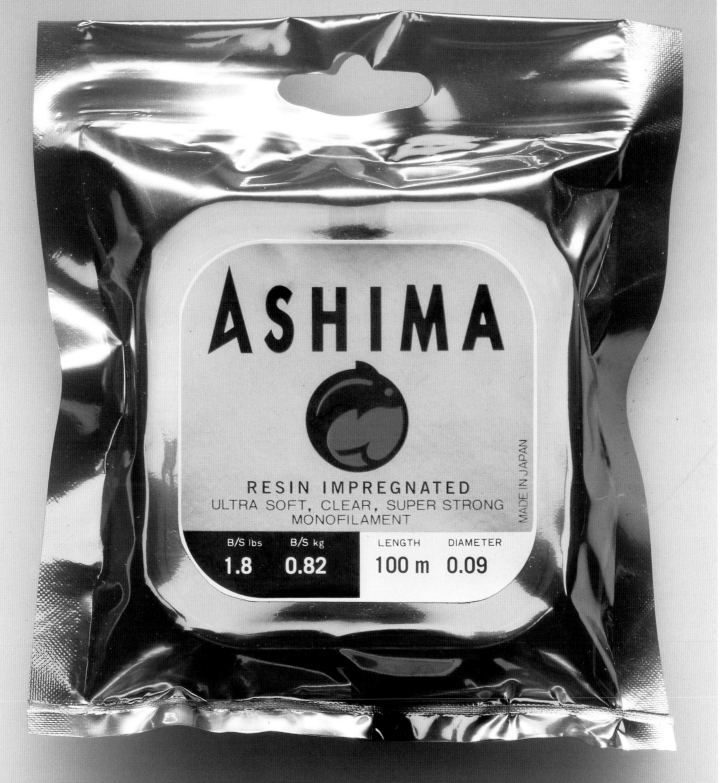

HALFORDS AUTOMOTIVE ACCESSORIES

DESIGNER Harry Pearce
ART DIRECTOR Harry Pearce, Domenic Lippa
COPYWRITER Giles Calver
DESIGN GROUP Lippa Pearce Design Ltd
CLIENT/MANUFACTURER Halfords

Lippa Pearce were asked to redesign all
Halfords' aerials and accessory products
as part of the total re-evaluation of the
Halfords brand. The accessories range
had to complement the core range but at
the same time have maximum individual
on-shelf impact.
The designers chose a neutral background
of grey to help project the actual products.
A strong, informative illustration was then
incorporated into the front face, showing
how the product worked.

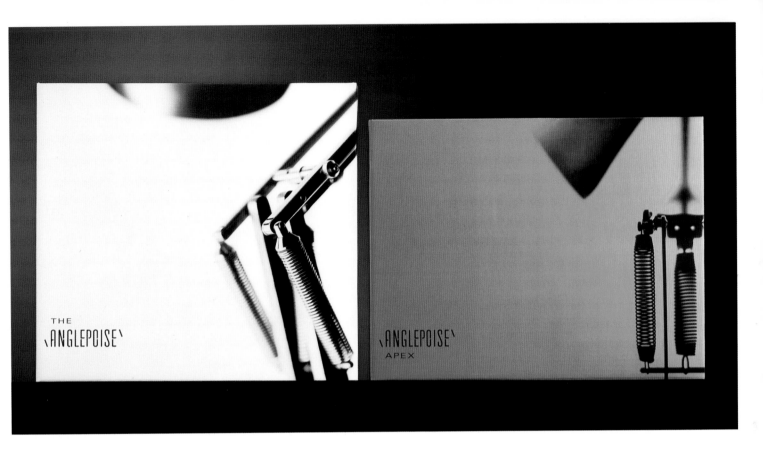

ANGLEPOISE DESK LAMP

DESIGNER David Beard
ART DIRECTOR Mark Wickens
PHOTOGRAPHERS Robin Broadbent,
John Pickering
DESIGN GROUP Wickens Tutt Southgate
CLIENT/MANUFACTURER Anglepoise Ltd

Designed at the beginning of the century,
the Anglepoise lamp is based on the human
arm. The classic mechanics of the simple
idea enable the lamp to be positioned in any
way with perfect balance. The packaging for
Anglepoise focuses on the mechanics and not
the fact that it is a lamp. The Anglepoise
logo is loosely based around the spring which
is integral to the lamp's mechanism.

DESIGNERS Mary Lewis,
Shaun Bowen, Ann Marshall
ART DIRECTOR Mary Lewis
PHOTOGRAPHY
Christopher Ridley, David Gill
ILLUSTRATION David Worth, Line & Line
DESIGN GROUP Lewis Moberly
CLIENT/MANUFACTURER Halfords Ltd

Halfords is an accessible retail chain
selling products for all motorists' needs.
There are nine products in their range
of torches. The packaging aims to convey
the situation in which the particular
torch would be useful. For example,
Hazard lamps are for when your car
breaks down and Multifunctional lamps
are free-standing. The overall feel is
appropriately dark with the torch itself
being the only source of light.
The information focuses on the benefits
of each product, avoiding repetition and
encouraging cross-purchasing as a
collectable set.

Compact Camera Outfit **with Motor Drive**

200MD

Including:
case, film,
battery
and two year
guarantee

Camera Outfit **with Fixed Focus**

100FF

Including:
case, film,
battery
and two year
guarantee

Camera Outfit **with Auto Focus**

300AF

Including:
case, film,
battery
and two year
guarantee

F5.6 30mm

Camera Outfit **with Multi Zoom**

Including:
case, film,
battery
and two year
guarantee

BOOTS CAMERAS

DESIGNERS Michael Denny, Andrew Ross,
Deborah Osborne, Jeremy Roots
ART DIRECTOR John Bateson
PHOTOGRAPHER John Summerhayes
DESIGN GROUP Roundel Design Group,
CLIENT/MANUFACTURER Boots The Chemist

Roundel Design Group were commissioned
to create new packaging and camera graphics
for this range of own-brand camera packs.
The packaging had to reinforce the company's
core values of trust, expertise and quality.
The graphics reflect the gift status of the
camera and work across all the products in
an expanding range.

FINITY ARTIST'S ACRYLICS RANGE

DESIGNERS Brian Green, Sharon Crossman
ART DIRECTOR Brian Green
PHOTOGRAPHER Andy Seymour
DESIGN GROUP The Green House
CLIENT/MANUFACTURER Windsor & Newton Ltd

The Green House were briefed to revitalise
and repackage all Windsor & Newton's Artist's
Acrylics Finity range and to develop a consistent
brand image for all products. The aim was to
reflect the personality of the brand and achieve
strong standout in competition with Windsor
& Newton's key competitors. Established in 1832,
Windsor & Newton's name is synonymous with
the finest art materials. In a highly competitive
market, with worldwide demand for acrylics
continuing to grow, the company has reformulated
its range of 75 colours, all of which feature the
purest of pigments to give the optimum brilliance
of colour. The new design features a still-life
showing the flexibility of acrylics used to evoke
emotion through a richness of colour and quality.

DESIGNERS Steve Hutton, Andrew Cuschieri,
Victoria Fenton, Graham Pritchard
ART DIRECTOR Steve Hutton
ILLUSTRATORS Andrew Cuschieri,
Victoria Fenton
DESIGN GROUP Hutton & Partners
CLIENT/MANUFACTURER
James Galt & Company

Galt Toys have an established reputation
for imaginative toys and crafts designed
for children aged up to ten years old.
Trusted by parents for their reputation for
quality, this project launched Galt into a
new sector: children's colouring materials.
Aimed at three to seven-year-olds, the
objective was to establish a European
brand with a strong shelf presence.
The range consists of 43 products, each
with six language descriptions on the back
of the pack. Hutton & Partners also designed
some of the products, such as the metal paint
box, play apron and splash mat.

The decision was made to display the bright
colours of the products themselves, whenever
possible, using cut out packs. Simple humorous
illustrations serve to convey the function and
unusual characteristics of the products to a
pan-European market. At the same time, aware
of parents' concerns for safety, the overall
design presents a range of products which can
be trusted.

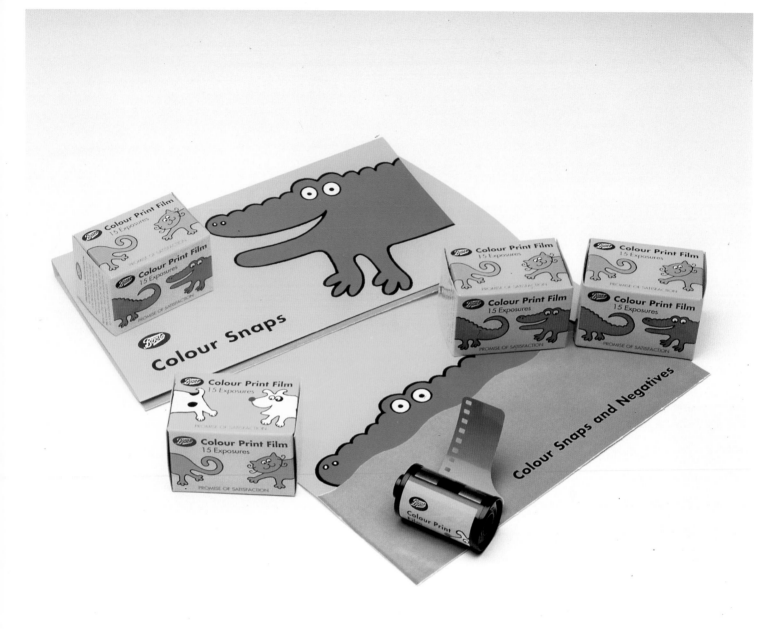

BOOTS FILM & PACK FOR CHILDREN

DESIGNER Lindsey Turnham
ART DIRECTOR Alan Colville
ILLUSTRATOR Sonia Canals
DESIGN GROUP Ian Logan Design Company
CLIENT/MANUFACTURER Boots The Chemist

Ian Logan's brief from Boots was to create an accessible, fun image that would make children feel at ease with the whole process of buying film, taking photographs and having them developed. One of the first decisions was to reduce the number of shots on the film to 12 or 15 in recognition of the impatience of children who want to see their photographs and show them to friends and family. The design solution uses primary colours and a strong cartoon style to heighten the difference from ordinary film and highlight the child's sense of ownership. A crocodile with open jaws gives

a humorous verbal link to 'snaps' which is familiar to children from story books; a cat and dog offer more domestic imagery, suggesting that the ordinary and everyday is worth capturing on film. Featuring the back and front halves of the animals rather than a fully-framed dog, cat and crocodile, helps make the packs more interesting, suggests movement and implicitly removes the proscriptions imposed by adults on what makes a good photograph. This allows children freedom to compose their own shots. It also evokes the comic strip, another familiar

and unthreatening reference, which underlines that taking photographs is fun! This simple pack design has been hugely successful, making an enormous impact on sales and winning awards in the UK, Europe and the USA.

PLAYSCHOOL LIL' LADY BUG

DESIGNER James Bell
ART DIRECTOR Judi Green
DESIGN GROUP The Green House
CLIENT/MANUFACTURER Hasbro Europe

The Green House was briefed to create
a range identity for the pan-European
pre-school toys 'Lil' Lady'. The design had
to work within the established Playschool
packaging, but differentiate the Lil' Lady
range. A new updated logo was created
incorporating a generic flower symbol that
would work on multi-lingual packs.
The final design features a subtle landscape
illustration of grass and flowers which
enhances the product photography and gives
the range its own personality and style.

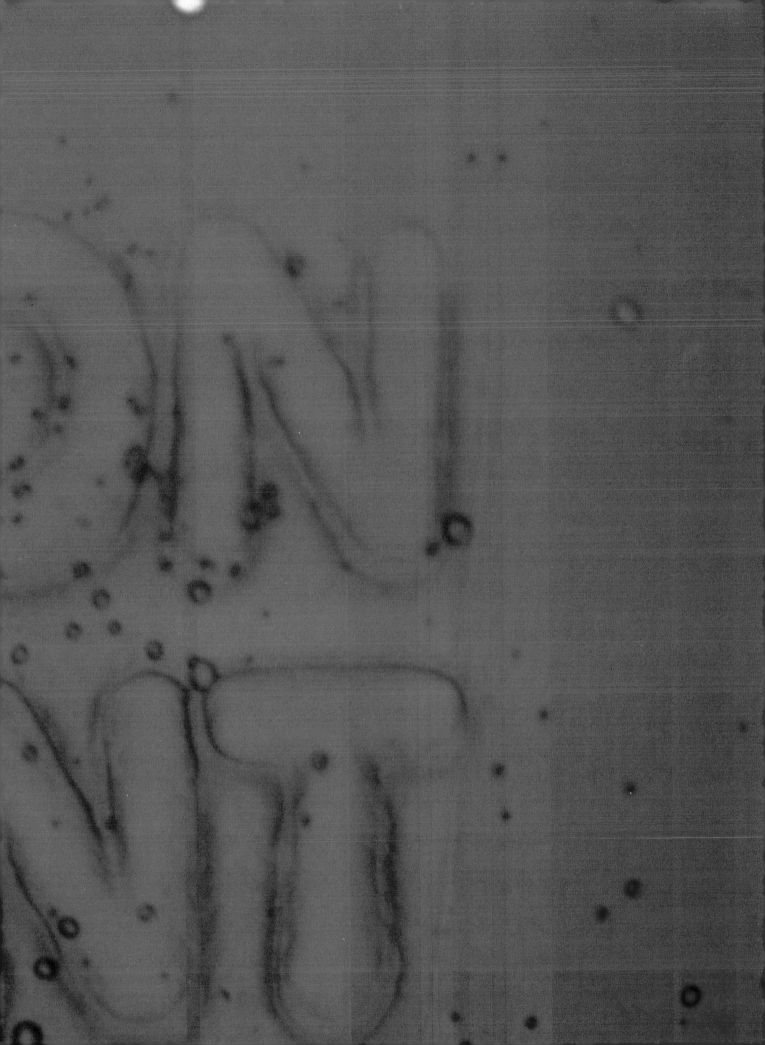

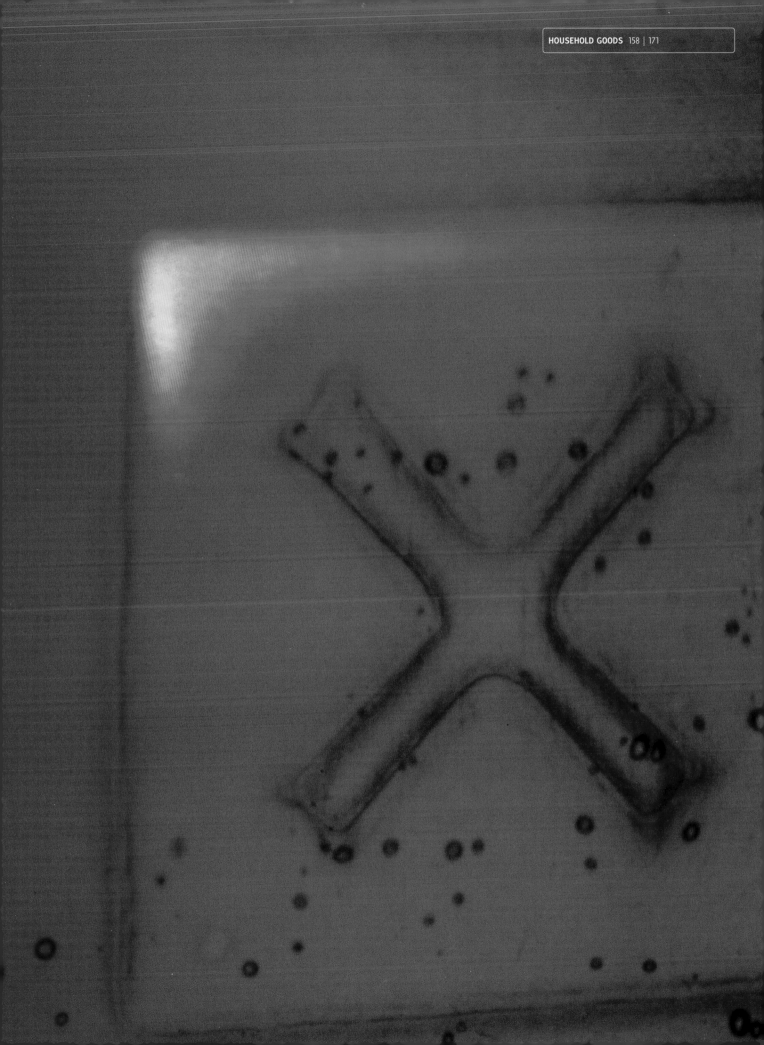

DESIGNERS Mary Lewis, Kasia Rust
ART DIRECTOR Mary Lewis
DESIGN GROUP Lewis Moberly
CLIENT/MANUFACTURER Boots The Chemist

The brief here was to create packaging for a
new range of laundry care products for Boots.
The design clearly communicates each type
of product by taking the universal washing
instruction symbols and making them
the hero of the pack. The design team aimed
to create a simple informative range which
would have a high impact on the shelf
and reflect the caring qualities of Boots.

DESIGNER/ART DIRECTOR Deborah Biggins
DESIGN GROUP Light & Coley
CLIENT/MANUFACTURER Windsor & Newton

The objective here was to launch a quality
range of acrylic colour products for students
under the Windsor & Newton name. The aim
was to increase Windsor & Newton's share
of the growing acrylic market and project
a strong, impactful look across the range.
The acrylics sector of colourants are aimed
at a reasonably young market with little
heritage. The market has been growing over
a number of years targeting student, amateur
and professional artists working on a large
scale, with economy in mind. The product
range includes 25 colours in competitively
priced 500ml squeezy pots. The specification
of the product was rapid drying, simple to
use, low odour, waterproof with good adhesive
qualities. Labels were to be in three colours
and four languages. The solution was to
develop a memorable name which would
be understood across language barriers,
establish strong brand identity and create
maximum shelf-impact by allowing the
colour itself to show through the label.

DULUX PAINT RANGE

DESIGN GROUP Coley Porter Bell
CLIENT/MANUFACTURER ICI Paints

Dulux is the brand leader in the paint market.
Over the last five years Coley Porter Bell
has been helping to manage the growth and
development of its identity across the world.
Recently CPB was asked to protect Dulux's
market-leading status from the increasing
threat of own-label brands through a new
look that is totally unique to the paint
market. The brief covered two principal
points. First, to create a truly distinctive
design which could be legally trademarked
and registered. Second, to make the brand
more contemporary and consolidate Dulux's
core values. The new brand features the
distinctive Dulux dog, rendered in a flowing
illustration and appearing more dynamic
and contemporary than on previous packaging.

DENES HEALTHY LIFESTYLE PET CARE

DESIGNER/ART DIRECTOR John Blackburn
ILLUSTRATOR John Geary
DESIGN GROUP Blackburn's Ltd
CLIENT/MANUFACTURER
Denes Natural Pet Care

Although the concept of a healthy diet
and natural foods for pets was introduced
as long ago as 1961, the products have
been available only through mail order
or specialist shops. When Denes sought
to build a wider distribution base in
the supermarket multiples, a total
redesign was needed. The skipping dog
and cat instantly communicate the
proposition with very effective standout
in this crowded, predictable sector.
The design is individual, distinctive and
well suited to a high quality independent
brand in a mainstream environment.
It also underlines the premium price
and positive benefits of the product in
an immediate, friendly and relevant way.

DESIGNER Rebecca Foster
ART DIRECTOR Mike Dempsey
ILLUSTRATION
STANDARD RANGE Isabelle Dervaux
TOP QUALITY RANGE Sourced from Archives
DESIGN GROUP CDT Design
CLIENT/MANUFACTURER WH Smith Ltd

While WH Smith stocked a vast range
of stationery, customers often found it
difficult to make comparisons between
products packaged in a very similar way.
WH Smith asked CDT Design to develop
distinctive new looks for the covers
of pads, notebooks and exercise books
in five ranges, according to the type
of paper used. The objective was to help
customers select what they needed
quickly and easily. CDT Design convinced
WH Smith of the need to rewrite the brief.
Their previous ranges attempted to apply
one design idea across all five ranges,
which caused customer confusion.
Redefining just three categories, Smith's
Top Quality, Standard and Economy
ranges, CDT Design produced separate
designs for each. CDT Design analysed
the kind of people who would buy
the different categories of stationery,
focusing on the style of design with
which they would identify. Famous
writers, architects, fashion designers,
musicians and mathematicians were
chosen to appear on the front covers
of the Top Quality range.
For the Standard range, CDT Design
commissioned an illustrator to produce
faces for the covers which relate
to the users of the pads. Green and blue
backgrounds defined recycled and non-
recycled papers respectively.
The covers relate closely to the needs
and aspirations of customers - from
schoolchildren to accountants - making
them more desirable in commercial terms.

WH SMITH
Standard Pad
160 x A4 sheets. Plain paper

WH SMITH
Standard Pad
100 x A5 sheets. Narrow ruled with margin

WH SMITH
Notebook
88 pages. Narrow ruled

WH SMITH
Notebook
32 sheets. Narrow ruled

WH SMITH
Notepad
32 sheets. Narrow ruled

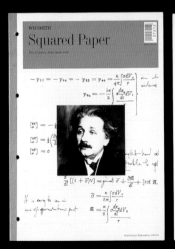

WH SMITH
Squared Paper

WH SMITH
Tracing Paper

WH SMITH
Graph Paper

WH SMITH
Fluorescent Paper

DESIGNER Rachel Shaw
ART DIRECTOR Glyn West
ILLUSTRATOR Pam English
DESIGN GROUP Nettle Design Ltd
CLIENT/MANUFACTURER Asda Stores Ltd

The Big Top range of kids' tissues forms part of a complete redesign of all Asda facial tissues. The brief was to introduce packs relevant for children that mothers would buy specifically for them.
The circus theme is carried through three different packs and features circus characters using tissues in comic ways. When empty, the packs can be cut up and children can play circus games with the characters.

LA CAFETIÈRE COFFEE MAKER

DESIGNER/ART DIRECTOR Alan Colville
PHOTOGRAPHER Simon Battersby
ILLUSTRATOR Computer Generated
DESIGN GROUP Ian Logan Design Company
CLIENT/MANUFACTURER Household Articles

The name 'La Cafetière' is a registered trademark owned by Household Articles. The designers' brief was to create packaging for a new cafetière designed by Queensbury Hunt for the student market. The solution is bold, colourful and simple. It uses hot, Mediterranean orange as the background colour with a bright blue cup to reinforce the continental colouring and give a suggestion of café society. These are also 'young' colours, seen a lot in club and sportswear fashions and in designer interiors. Linked photographs of the cafetière on three sides of the pack create a story: showing it being filled, coffee being poured and a full pot of coffee. Store staff were briefed to stack the packs in this way to ensure greater standout and present much more impact and interest to the consumer. This made it far more effective on shelf than the competition. The packaging helped the client break into many new outlets; its great success has encouraged them to redesign their existing pack.

TESCO GLASSWARE

DESIGNERS David Richmond, David Gray
ART DIRECTOR David Richmond
PHOTOGRAPHER James Murphy
DESIGN GROUP David Richmond Associates
CLIENT/MANUFACTURER Tesco

The brief here was to design the packaging
for a range of glassware for Tesco. The client
wanted the packaging to show the uses of
the different glasses within the range, and to
make use of the physical packaging supplied.
The designers used photography to link the
product itself, which is visible in the pack,
to the ways in which the glasses can be used,
with shots of different drinks in each glass.
The solution proved successful as it was
visually interesting and unusual, but at
the same time completely straightforward,
allowing the customer to actually see the
product in its package,

BOOTS HOME FRAGRANCE RANGE

DESIGNERS Brian Webb, Lynn Trickett, Colin Gifford
ART DIRECTOR Brian Webb, Lynn Trickett
ILLUSTRATOR Westcott Design
DESIGN GROUP Trickett & Webb Ltd
CLIENT/MANUFACTURER Boots The Chemist

The brief here was to package a range
of perfumed products for the home. These
included scented candles, pot pourri,
scented drawer liners and fresheners.
Trickett & Webb used the language of
home decoration by turning the labelling
into fabric swatches. Each fragrance
is identified with a fabric design:
floral, tartan, paisley and patchwork.
The labelling was pinked around the edges
in the traditional swatch method. Gift
selections were packaged in reuseable
mini carrier bags printed all over in the
relevant fabric design.

Inspired by traditional

Floral chintz fabrics...

Boots

FLORAL

this sachet is fragranced

with a perfume of subtle fruity

top notes which develop into

a heart of jasmine, tuberose

and gardenia, refined by

the scent of precious

woods and musk.

Inspired by the traditional

fabric Tartan...

Boots

TARTAN

this fragranced sachet evokes

the fresh Celtic moorlands

and the rich ancestry

of the Highlands. Combining

the evocative scent of

heather with warm

earthy elements.

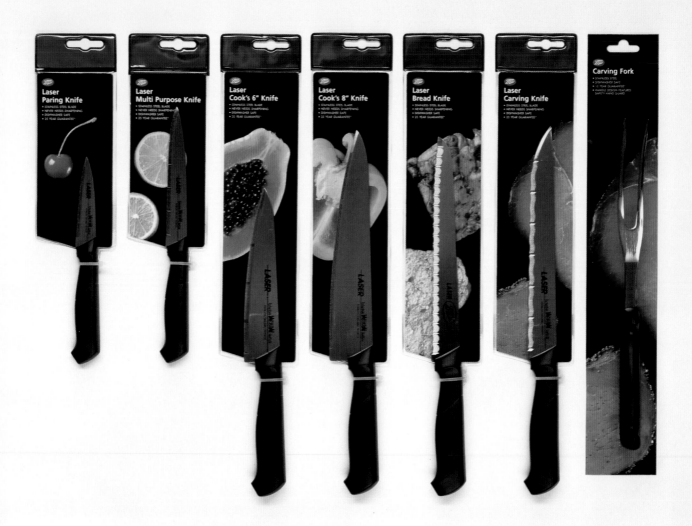

BOOTS COOKING KNIVES

DESIGNER/ART DIRECTOR Alan Colville
PHOTOGRAPHER Clive White
DESIGN GROUP Ian Logan Design Company
CLIENT/MANUFACTURER Boots The Chemist

The designers were asked by Boots to
approach the packaging of kitchenware
in a way that represented lifestyle rather
than utility. This reflects the importance
to Boots of this sector of the market and
their desire to place saucepans, cooking
utensils and accessories into the growing,
lucrative gift area. The designers used
fine foods photography, focusing on more
exotic ingredients on a plain, usually
black background, to create an exciting,
contemporary, high-quality feel.
The photography often continues on the
sides of packs to add further interest.
By creating an identifiable family of
products, the packaging encourages the
customer to buy more than one item.
Sales of kitchenware have increased
dramatically with the new packs.

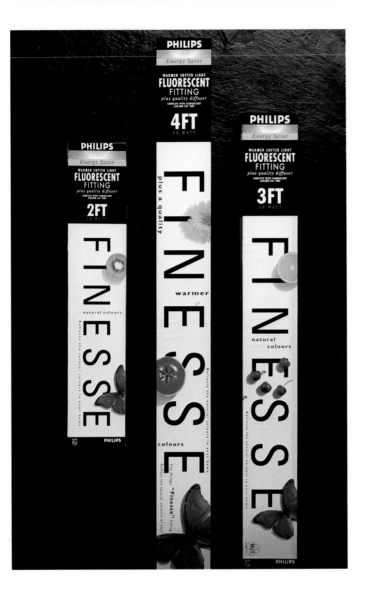

PHILIPS FINESSE LIGHTING

DESIGNER Garrick Hamm
ART DIRECTOR Glenn Tutssel
PHOTOGRAPHER Andy Seymour
DESIGN GROUP Tutssels
CLIENT/MANUFACTURER Philips

Finesse is a new product range offering
warmer, softer lighting from a fluorescent
fitting and a true colour in the home.
The challenge faced by Tutssels was
to demonstrate an innovative new product
range in what is a bland and fairly stagnant
market sector. The range includes a variety
of products with differing specifications.
The solution was to create a strong
brand recognition and clearly communicate
key product uses with distinctive icons.
The Finesse range is more up-market in
feel and, with its illustrations of natural
flowers, vegetables and the like, it quickly
communicates the core benefit of the brand's
natural lighting.

DESIGNERS Chrissie Charlton, Vicky Fullock
ART DIRECTOR Chrissie Charlton
ILLUSTRATOR Charlotte Knox
DESIGN GROUP Chrissie Charlton & Company
CLIENT/MANUFACTURER Royal Shibas Ltd

Royal Shibas, a company specialising in fine
and gourmet foods for the gift market in Japan,
required richly illustrated packaging for a range
of five preserves which includes unusual flavours
such as dandelion and rose petal. Chrissie
Charlton commissioned the artist Charlotte
Knox to produce tempera paintings of the seven
flavours which were then used on labels and
gift boxes. The result is a high quality packaging
system that utilizes the bright colours and rich
textures of the artwork for maximum shelf-impact.

DESIGNER Jan Atkins
ART DIRECTOR Alan Colville
ILLUSTRATOR Corinna Reetz
DESIGN GROUP Ian Logan Design Company
CLIENT/MANUFACTURER Whittard of Chelsea

Ian Logan has an extremely close and successful relationship with Whittard of Chelsea, for whom they have designed packaging for dozens of tea and coffee ranges and also a range of biscuit tins. Approaching this commission to package a range of preserves, the designers wanted to reflect the innovative identity they had already devised for Whittard. All packs are designed to be seen in a progressive retail environment and aim to encourage experimentation and the desire amongst customers to collect them.

The creamy-yellow background of the new jam labels has a crackle finish which it to the biscuit tins, helping to stir the customers' interest in extending their collections. The name of each preserve is scripted as if handwritten, which adds to the feeling that one is buying from small batch production, almost as if it were home made. The illustrations are again contemporary in feeling and deeply coloured and textured, giving the fruit depth and making it look luscious and juicy. The packs have been highly successful and have helped create a collector culture amongst Whittard's customers.

HARTLEY'S PURE FRUIT JAMS

DESIGNERS Neal Dodge, Antonia Hayward
ART DIRECTOR Rod Petrie
ILLUSTRATOR Charlotte Knox
DESIGN GROUP Design Bridge Ltd
CLIENT/MANUFACTURER Chivers Hartley

Hartley's Pure Fruit Jams was an existing
brand which boasted a unique cooking process
that sealed in the flavour. The earlier pack
did not exploit this theme, so the design task
here centred on the communication of real fruit
flavours. In order to achieve this a 'fruity' cap
design was created which not only frees up the
front label but also forms a design equity for
the product range. The front label features a
simple illustration of the fruit and the overall
look is reminiscent of a homemade jam label,
emphasising the purity of the product. Hartley's
was one of the first companies to pioneer the
tamper seal, which lent itself ideally to the
real fruit and homemade theme of the product.

DESIGNER Domenic Lippa
ART DIRECTOR Harry Pearce, Domenic Lippa
ILLUSTRATOR Jane Human
DESIGN GROUP Lippa Pearce Design Ltd
CLIENT/MANUFACTURER Waitrose

Chutneys derive from recipes brought back from
the East in the 18th and 19th centuries. These
recipes, now accepted as almost quintessentially
English, have been joined in more recent years
by more exotic varieties from other parts of
the globe. The designers' brief was to create
labelling for Waitrose's chutney range which
would distinguish between the flavours and be
stylish enough for consumers to feel comfortable
about placing the jars on their tables.
Chutney has a rich, textured quality that speaks
for itself, so labels were deliberately designed
to identify the product rather than overdress it.
Background colours and distinctive illustrations
of the natural products serve to differentiate
the recipes. Hand-drawn lettering suggests
the historical roots of the chutneys by being
suggestive of handmade, country produce.

ARRAN FINE FOODS

DESIGNERS Ron Burnett,
Jack Rodgers, Suzanne Aylott
ART DIRECTOR Ron Burnett
ILLUSTRATORS Ean Taylor,
Ros Fowler, Bridgette Collins
DESIGN GROUP Graphic Partners
CLIENT/MANUFACTURER Pateron Arran Ltd.

The repositioning of the Arran Brand involved
the design of a new logo to echo the geometry
of the jars, a redesign of their five-year-old
packaging, with new graphics for the lids and
tamper-evident seals, and new labels to create
three distinct identities for the three various
ranges.
The creative work recently won a prestigious
Clio International Design Award in New York.

DESIGNER/ART DIRECTOR Brian Delaney
ILLUSTRATOR Sue Williams, Folio
DESIGN GROUP Delaney Design Consultants
CLIENT/MANUFACTURER Waitrose Ltd

Shelf impact, strong use of colour and ease of
product identification within the range were key
points in this Waitrose brief for a range of Bio
and Diet Bio yogurts. Each pack consists of four
pots and an outer sleeve. The designers chose
a strong colourful illustration style for the fruit,
with different coloured foregrounds for each
sleeve. Individual pot background colours match
the corresponding sleeve. The illustration style
is suitable for both flexographic and litho-
graphic printing while a simple colour change
to the type differentiates Bio and Diet Bio
products within the range.

DESIGNER Tim Leslie-Smith
ART DIRECTOR Robin Hall
ILLUSTRATOR Tim Leslie-Smith
DESIGN GROUP Davies Hall
CLIENT/MANUFACTURER Biogreen

This quality drinking yogurt was selling well
in certain stores but was particularly targeted
at the Asian market, who are large consumers
of yogurt. Biogreen wanted to broaden its
target market without alienating its large
Asian market.
Davies Hall were asked to design a convincing
quality brand. The bold badge device gives
Biogreen a strong brand identity. The 'milky'
cow illustration and bright colours used on
a white background with a certain fun fruitiness
give the product an individual personality.

ASDA FRENCH SET YOGURT

DESIGNER: Daniel Gallimore
ART DIRECTOR Martin Seymour
DESIGN GROUP Light & Coley
CLIENT/MANUFACTURER Asda Group

The objective in this case was to introduce
a new whole milk yogurt range into the
luxury sector of the market. This was to
replace the low fat and very low fat lines
and to take advantage of a sector which
had no dominant brands. The brief was to
communicate the French authenticity of
the product and to reflect the thick and
creamy whole milk qualities in the design.
The product was launched as a six pack
and twelve pot multi-pack. Light & Coley
created richness on the pack through
a flowing French flag and hand-crafted
typography. The thick and creamy nature
was conveyed with a silky texture on the
flag and through the text.
The design also created impact with
multiple facings with the flowing wave.

MD MILKS

DESIGNER Belinda Duggan
ART DIRECTOR John Blackburn
ILLUSTRATOR John Geary
DESIGN GROUP Blackburn's Ltd
CLIENT/MANUFACTURER MD Foods plc

This new design creates a strong branding
for MD Milks through the use of simple
emotive graphics featuring a cow sniffing
at buttercups. The brand is also separated
from its competitors through the use of bold
colours which make it stand out in a market
dominated by white packs. This also creates
a clear differentiation between this particular
product and others in a range of milks and
creams.

HARVEY NICHOLS
PANETTONE

Michael Nash Associates were asked
to create an identity for Harvey Nichols
own-brand food. This was a new venture
for both the designers and the client.
The designers had never tackled food
packaging before; Harvey Nichols had
never sold food. Obviously, the designers
did not have to compete with the major
supermarkets, but Harvey Nichols' food
would be seen alongside familiar brands.
All the designers' thoughts centred on
the existing Harvey Nichols customer
and ideas about what they might want.
Their simple concept was to package the
food as if it were a silk scarf, provoking
a design solution which is based around
the feelings or sensations that various
foods give us, as opposed to a literal
representation of the product.
Harvey Nichols supported the concept
with unfailing confidence.
The results speak for themselves:

HARVEY NICHOLS PANATONE

DESIGNERS
Stephanie Nash, Anthony Michael
ART DIRECTORS
Stephanie Nash, Anthony Michael
PHOTOGRAPHER Toby Glanville
DESIGN GROUP Michael Nash Associates
CLIENT/MANUFACTURER Harvey Nichols

Panatone, for example, is Italy's Christmas
cake. So this image, shot by Toby Glanville,
evokes a combination of a special treat
cake with a more general Italian scene.

HARVEY NICHOLS SUN DRIED TOMATOES AND PASTA

DESIGNERS Stephanie Nash,
Teresa Roviras, Anthony Michael
ART DIRECTORS
Stephanie Nash, Anthony Michael
PHOTOGRAPHER Toby Glanville
DESIGN GROUP Michael Nash Associates
CLIENT/MANUFACTURER Harvey Nichols

In this instance, a typical Italian feel
is the key to the photographic theme for
the Italian foods. Thoughts of appetising
pasta conjure up images of Naples.
The street scene also offers a slightly
tongue-in-cheek view of romantic Italy.

HARVEY NICHOLS OILS AND VINEGAR

DESIGNERS Stephanie Nash,
Teresa Roviras, Anthony Michael
ART DIRECTORS
Stephanie Nash, Anthony Michael
PHOTOGRAPHER Matthew Donaldson
DESIGN GROUP Michael Nash Associates
CLIENT/MANUFACTURER Harvey Nichols

In this case, the idea is to exploit
the viscosity and good quality of
Harvey Nichols' olive oil and the
sharp, more fluid quality of vinegar.
The oils are differentiated not only
by image but by bottle shape,
creating interest within the range
and therefore encouraging
collectability. The design is strong
whether the bottles are seen
independently or together as a range.

HARVEY NICHOLS

OLIVE OIL

750ml e 25.3floz

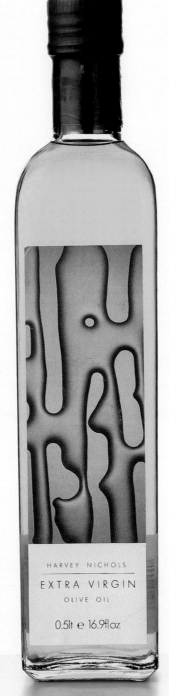

HARVEY NICHOLS

EXTRA VIRGIN

OLIVE OIL

0.5lt e 16.9floz

HARVEY NICHOLS

PROVENCE
HERB
VINEGAR
6°

net
ct. 8½floz 25cl e

OSCAR SAMUEL OLIVE OILS

DESIGNER Jayne Connell
ART DIRECTOR Nick Downes
PHOTOGRAPHER Spiros Politis Photography
DESIGN GROUP Carter Wong & Partners
CLIENT/MANUFACTURER
Philip Britten, Oscar Samuels

A stylish and tasteful brand identity was needed
for these speciality virgin olive oils, each one
infused with a distinctive flavour and created by
Philip Britten, Michelin Star chef at the Capital
Hotel. In creating the brand identity, everything
from the choice of bottles to the method of
displaying the labels was considered. The design
was inspired by the work of Spiros Politis, a
photographer well known for his brightly coloured
shots of people. Applying his style to food results
in crisp packaging which stands apart from its
competition, while sandblasting the Oscar Samuel
logo onto the glass creates a subtle but permanent
branding device.

KOMILI OILS

DESIGNERS Wendy Mellors,
Mark Bedden, Kevin Greene
ART DIRECTORS Karen House, Peter Kay
ILLUSTRATOR Harry Willcock, London
DESIGN GROUP Design Bridge Ltd
CLIENT/MANUFACTURER Unilever Turkey

While Komili is Turkey's biggest edible oil brand, a decline in olive oil consumption in Turkey highlighted the need to communicate with younger users. The new target for Komili was seen as those who understand the health values of olive oil. Design Bridge had the opportunity to enhance the image of Komili olive oil as a premium, natural and contemporary product through fresh graphics and a new bottle structure. The resulting label design features a beautifully illustrated olive whose shape is reflected structurally on the side of the bottle. The oval-shaped 'hole' through the center of the bottle provides a more interesting and practical holding device, thus enabling easier pouring. In addition, the designers were able to work closely with Komili's suppliers, providing Alias generated digital data to ensure time and cost savings. Specifically, their design resulted in a 20% increase in sales, with little additional marketing support, as well as a 30% reduction in production costs.

AMOY SAUCES

DESIGN DIRECTOR Andrew King
CREATIVE DIRECTOR Richard Ford
DESIGN GROUP Landor Associates
CLIENT/MANUFACTURER BE International Ltd

Amoy and Lotus were two respected ingredient and food brands in Oriental cuisine. Both had roots which lay deep in south-east Asia and, although they had differing brand equities, they essentially shared the same product base. The existence of both brands made little sense to its parent company, BE Inter national, as they were becoming lost in a growing array of strong competitors. It was felt by BE International that the Amoy and Lotus brands would be better served if they were consolidated under the stronger Amoy identity. Combining the two brands under the umbrella of the Amoy identity required sensitivity towards the heritage and authenticity of both brands, while maximising the authority and impact needed to compete effectively with established western brands. With the international market continuing to expand rapidly, the design system also had to be flexible in order to allow further extensions of the brand into new sectors, such as frozen dim sum. The Amoy identity was strengthened through the use of a golden ribbon device inspired by the ubiquitous use of ribbons throughout south-east Asian cultures. The system reflects the richness and quality of the cuisine through creative combination of colour and texture. The design positions Amoy as a discerning, ambassadorial brand that represents the true taste of Asia. Within eight months of its relaunch, the Amoy brand achieved leadership in the soy sauce market.

TWININGS AROMATIC TEAS

DESIGNER Nigel Grey
ART DIRECTOR Alison Tomlin
ILLUSTRATOR Bob Haberfield
DESIGN GROUP Carter Wong & Partners
CLIENT/MANUFACTURER R Twining & Co

This new packaging for Twinings Aromatic Teas evolved from an existing range developed to compete with the arrival of new brands such as Liptons and Pickwick. At the same time, it was designed to convey the rich fruity taste and aroma of the teas. The teas are retailed on a pan-European basis. To enhance the message of fresh, fruity flavours, the colours of the packs were made stronger and deeper while the illustrator, Bob Haberfield, was briefed to createidealised versions of the fruits in the range, exaggerating their qualities to convey the taste of the product. The design reflects Twinings' heritage and the company's perceived images of quality and reliability. The range includes 11 different flavours which are retailed across Europe.

WHISTLESTOP TEA AND ESPRESSO COFFEE

DESIGNERS Paul Davis,
Russell Howorth, Virginia Armstrong
ART DIRECTOR Paul Davis
ILLUSTRATOR Russell Howorth
DESIGN GROUP Agenda Design Associates
CLIENT/MANUFACTURER Whistlestop Café

Agenda Design Associates were commissioned
by Whistlestop Café to create a range of
own-label products. The tea and coffee packs
featured here form part of a family for the
Whistlestop portfolio and mark a move away
from the traditional language used by main
brand products in the sector. The use of
distinctive illustrations linked to the
contrasting linear format of the pack creates
a memorable and appealing product identity.

DESIGNER/ART DIRECTOR Marcello Minale
DESIGN GROUP Minale, Tattersfield & Partners Ltd
CLIENT/MANUFACTURER San Pellegrino

Minale, Tattersfield & Partners redesigned the
Splendid range of coffee, currently the second
biggest coffee brand in Italy, for Kraft Jacob
Suchard and the European market; this included
the development of a new logotype.
The range consists of six variations of flavour -
Classico, Moka, Moka Forte, Night & Day, Riserva
Oro - and the full range consists of nearly 35 packs.

TORZ & MACATONIA COFFEE PACKAGING

ART DIRECTORS Harry Pearce & Domenic Lippa
DESIGNER Paul Tunnicliffe
COPYWRITER Giles Calver
DESIGN GROUP Lippa Pearce Design Ltd
CLIENT/MANUFACTURER Torz & Macatonia

Jeremy Torz and Steven Macatonia's company
aims to supply quality coffee freshly roasted
and dispatched within 24 hours of an order
being received. The designers developed the
name using the owners' surnames and a logotype
which both emphasizes the quality aspect of
their company as well as the richness of their
product. A seal device was produced which was
then applied to the letterheads, company
brochure and packaging. The seal reaffirms
the historical nature of coffee packaging.
The direct mail package utilises natural
materials to give the device a distinctive
appearance.

PERCOL INSTANT CAPPUCCINO

DESIGNER/ART DIRECTOR Glyn West
ILLUSTRATOR Peter Ross
DESIGN GROUP Nettle Design Ltd
CLIENT/MANUFACTURER
Brian Chapman Food Brands Group

The brief here was to produce packaging for
an addition to the Percol brand range of
instant and fresh coffees. Cappuccino entered
a growing speciality sector and was the first
to be packaged in Britain in a resealable drum.
Graphics were designed to present the product
as both stylish and modern whilst employing
colour references to its Italian associations.

HARVEY NICHOLS BAGUETTE BAGS

DESIGNER
Stephanie Nash
ART DIRECTORS
Stephanie Nash, Anthony Michael
DESIGN GROUP
Michael Nash Associates
CLIENT/MANUFACTURER
Harvey Nichols

As with all the Harvey Nichols food packaging, the inspiration for the idea comes from a feeling of what the food is, rather than a literal image of the food itself. Bread makes us think of ripened wheat which leads, in turn, to blue skies, which evoke images of freshness.

HOMEPRIDE COOKING SAUCES

DESIGNER John Ewles
ART DIRECTOR Ian Ritchie
DESIGN GROUP Jones Knowles Ritchie
CLIENT/MANUFACTURER
Campbell Grocery Products Ltd

The Deep South range is part of the
Homepride Cook In Sauce range.
The entire range was originally colour
coded by variant. However, the range is
so extensive it lacked any strong branding
and had little presence in its crowded
sector. The solution to this problem was
to make more of the Homepride blue by
using it to create a wall of colour which
immediately signals the brand. With this
established, the designers were able to
create individual sub-brands in which the
graphics reflect the personalities of the
various products. The Deep South brand's
more modern graphics reflect its contemporary personality.

BROOKE BOND RAGU SAUCE

DESIGNER/ART DIRECTOR David Pike
ILLUSTRATOR Richard Bonson
DESIGN GROUP Design Bridge Ltd
CLIENT/MANUFACTURER
Brooke Bond Foods Ltd

Although the existing Ragu packaging
communicated authenticity and quality,
it lacked brand personality and failed to
differentiate products within its own range.
In addition, when Ragu jars were stacked
next to rival sauce jars, they looked smaller.
Design Bridge developed an arched label
reflecting the personality of the Ragu
brand and enlarged the logo type. These
two elements combined to create improved
shelf impact while also addressing the size
problem. Appetite appeal and Ragu's
Italian-ness were improved through new
illustrations of the cooking scene - a key
brand symbol - and of fresh, quality ingredients as are central to the Ragu brand.
Functional product descriptors were replaced
by a banner device to give the label more
exuberance and improved variety definition.
In line with the brief, a strong sense of con -
tinuity with the original packs was maintained.

TESCO'S PASSION CAKE

DESIGNERS Chen Tsoi, Kara Sims
ART DIRECTOR Chen Tsoi
ILLUSTRATOR Terry Hand
DESIGN GROUP Chen Tsoi Design
CLIENT/MANUFACTURER Tesco Stores Ltd

When Tesco asked Chen Tsoi to package a range of American-influenced desserts, the brief specified that the design had to be versatile enough to accommodate further products to be added to the range later. A pop-art style of illustration was used to evoke the feel of an American diner. A cut-out window on the box showed the actual cake, incorporating it as a part of the illustration. Each product name was strongly branded in its own distinctive band of colour.

SCHWARTZ AUTHENTIC MIX RANGE

DESIGNER Brian Green
ART DIRECTOR Judi Green
PHOTOGRAPHER Chris Bailey
ILLUSTRATOR Brian Sweet
DESIGN GROUP The Green House
CLIENT/MANUFACTURER McCormick Foods

The Green House was briefed to redesign the entire Schwartz Authentic Mix range. With growing consumer interest in foreign and more exotic foods, the Schwartz range now includes 30 different recipes in three sub ranges: Traditional; Pasta Italia (featured here); and World Cuisine. The design objectives called for a differentiation between the three sub-brands without detracting from McCormick's international brand identity, as well as a clear and distinctive brand image conveying both the confidence and quality appropriate to a Schwartz product. Legibility and clear communication were also important. In a highly competitive market, the new design needed to maximise the potential on the brand through impact on the shelf and appetite appeal. The final design features products shot on different coloured gel backgrounds which were used to identify the recipe areas; green, for example, for Italian dishes. The central oval uses strong graphic illustrations which complement the illustrations for each sub-brand.

DESIGNER Rachel Shaw
ART DIRECTOR Glyn West
PHOTOGRAPHER Alan Marsh
ILLUSTRATOR Peter Ross
DESIGN GROUP Nettle Design Ltd
CLIENT/MANUFACTURER Tesco Stores Ltd

Tesco Deluxe Light Meat Tuna Steak is specially selected from fish caught in the seas around the island of St. Helena in the South Atlantic. The product is more expensive than standard tuna. It has been packaged in a carton to differentiate it and allow for strong graphics, establishing the heritage and background of St. Helena, as well as showing serving suggestions.

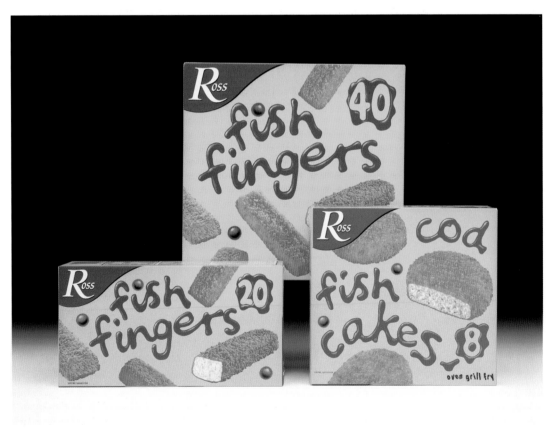

ROSS BREADED FISH RANGE

DESIGNER Nicola Sloan
ART DIRECTOR Alan Snell
PHOTOGRAPHER Chris Turner
ILLUSTRATOR Richard Duckett
DESIGN GROUP Springett Associates
CLIENT/MANUFACTURER Young's

Well-known for its broad range of everyday frozen food products, Ross has been a Springett Associates client for over 18 years. The brand is now owned by Young's. As the structure of the client organization has changed in pursuit of new strategies, Springett's has consistently worked to ensure the long-term health of the brand. Their ongoing brief is to build increasing recognition for Ross and achieve visual dominance over competitors in the freezer cabinet through directness and excellence of product presentation. Recently, Springett Associates worked with the client to reassess consumer propositions for all the Ross ranges, rationalising them into more contemporary offers. For example, this collection of breaded fish products is now repositioned as a children's range. Highly visible in the freezer cabinet, its evocative, fun representation of commodity products has given them a new lease of life.

WHITWORTHS SOUPS

DESIGNER Irina Roffe
ART DIRECTOR Jonathan Ford
PHOTOGRAPHER Alan Newnham
DESIGN GROUP Pearlfisher
International Design Partnership
CLIENT/MANUFACTURER Whitworths Ltd

For Whitworths, the old image of cooking
with beans and pulses was perceived by many
younger consumers as either too complicated,
vegetarian only, or just plain boring.
So a radical redesign was required to present
their beans and pulses in a more inspirational
light. The designers' idea hinges on the
creation of a contemporary look, built around
brightly colour-coded split plates, presenting
appetising dishes and serving suggestions.

TESCO TOMATO & HERB SOUPS

DESIGNERS David Richmond, David Gray
ART DIRECTOR David Richmond
PHOTOGRAPHER Paul Kemp, Chalcott Studios
ILLUSTRATOR Simon Critchley, Rhodes Studio
DESIGN GROUP David Richmond Associates
CLIENT/MANUFACTURER Tesco

The Just Stir range of soups was introduced
by Tesco as a high quality instant soup.
The main thrust of the design brief centred
on the need to communicate firstly that the
soup is easy to make and, secondly, that it
is a quality product containing interesting
ingredients. This was achieved by illustrating
the easy steps involved in making the soup and
turning the illustrations into decorations
placed on the bowl itself; the bowl of soup
was then photographed alongside bright
tomatoes against a dark background, creating
a striking contrast and maximum impact on
the shelf.

FRAY BENTOS PIE FILLINGS

DESIGNER Louise Wardle
ART DIRECTOR Ian Ritchie
PHOTOGRAPHER Andy Seymour
DESIGN GROUP Jones Knowles Ritchie
CLIENT/MANUFACTURER
Campbell Grocery Products Ltd

Despite being the brand leader in its sector,
successive redesigns over the last decade
had weakened the Fray Bentos brand identity
to the point where it had an imitative
appearance. By recalling the butcher's tiling
from early Fray Bentos advertising, the new
design draws on the brand's long heritage and
combines traditional elements with
contemporary styling. The overall effect has
heightened the product's shelf presence and
given it a wholesome, high quality identity.

DESIGNER
Simon Lince
ART DIRECTOR
Vanessa Fristedt
DESIGN GROUP
Michael Peters Ltd
CLIENT/MANUFACTURER
Bongrain Italia Spa

Michael Peters Limited developed the name and package design for this new cheese from the leading international cheese manufacturer, Bongrain. Torrigiano is positioned as an Italian cheese with Tuscan origins. All elements of the product, the name and packaging are intended to give the brand immediate authenticity. Drawing on traditional Italian imagery, and using a Leonardo Da Vinci illustration style, the packaging has been designed not only to give the whole product maximum stand out but also to retain brand recognition when the cheese is divided into sections at the point of purchase.

DESIGNERS Denise Pardey, Patrick Devlin
ART DIRECTOR Gerard O'Dwyer
PHOTOGRAPHY Patrice De Villiers
DESIGN GROUP The London Design Partnership Ltd
CLIENT/MANUFACTURER MacEwen Falconer

MacEwen Falconer have owned the Golden Acre
brand since the mid-1970s. The brand was sold
mainly as a catering range of products. Recently
the company decided to extend the Golden Acre
market and to make the brand primarily a retail
one. The redesign involved creating the GA logo.
The background colour is based on the original
dark blue of the existing packaging.
However, the designers selected a much more
vivid blue printed on a photographic background
of crushed paper to give a dramatic dimension
against the beautifully and simply photographed
pastas, fruits and vegetables. The combination
of vivid blue and green gives Golden Acre a very
strong, clear and recognisable identity. Since the
redesign the range has been successfully sold into
all the major multiples.

DESIGNER Sarah Roberts
Art Director Gary Cooke
ILLUSTRATORS Gary Cooke
DESIGN GROUP Horseman Cooke
CLIENT/MANUFACTURER Makro

Flour is one of Makro's basic commodities
sold in relatively small 3kg bags as well
as large sacks weighing up to 10kg.
Horseman Cooke's design had to be bold and
eye-catching, with an economic use of colour.
The illustration of a jolly chef with his hat
flying off is used as a brand device which
interacts with the title on the self-raising
packaging. The resulting image is simple
enough to work on the wide range of sizes
yet strong enough to stand out in the store.

DESIGNERS David Richmond, Neil Wood
ART DIRECTOR David Richmond
PHOTOGRAPHER Paul Kemp
DESIGN GROUP David Richmond Associates
CLIENT/MANUFACTURER Somerfield

Somerfield's brief for this project was part of the packaging redesign for all their own-label ice cream products. The sorbets, considered to be a luxury, are slightly more expensive than the other desserts in the range. The designers drew their inspiration from the work of photographers such as Irving Penn. The sorbets were sculpted into tulip shapes and photographed against a rich, dark back- ground to create a dramatic and elegant image. Each flower shape uses the natural colour of the product to create its personality, making it easy for the customer to identify the flavour in the package.

HEALTHY TIMES BABY CEREALS

DESIGNER/ART DIRECTOR Tricia Shiel
ILLUSTRATOR Diane Fisher
DESIGN GROUP Shiel Humphrey Design
CLIENT/MANUFACTURER Healthy Times

Healthy Times of San Diego have to compete in a market dominated by large, well established US baby food manufacturers. It was therefore important for their packaging to have unique shelf appeal. Through the use of illustrations resembling an illustrated children's book, the natural food aspect is highlighted by farmyard themes. Farm animals are one of the first things children learn about, so parents have a fun subject to talk about while feeding their children a delicious healthy cereal. A different illustration is used for each pack. Combined with colour coding, this helps distinguish between the three different flavours. This range has also been adapted to the Canadian market, where French and English texts have to live alongside each other. The baby cereal range is part of an expanding collection of Healthy Times products on sale in the USA, Canada, Australia and Japan.

DESIGN GROUP Newell and Sorrell Ltd
ILLUSTRATOR Tania Hurt-Newton
CLIENT/MANUFACTURER Boots The Chemist

These packs - part of Boots' range of healthy
foods for toddlers - were designed to be
as much fun for children as possible while
reassuring parents that the meals they
contain are highly nutritious. The packs turn
into serving trays with bright and amusing
illustrations designed to keep toddlers happy
while they have their meals.

DESIGNER Harry Pearce, Domenic Lippa
ART DIRECTORS Harry Pearce, Domenic Lippa
PHOTOGRAPHER Richard Foster
DESIGN GROUP Lippa Pearce Design Ltd
CLIENT/MANUFACTURER Boots The Chemist

The Shapers range consists of over a hundred dietary products and represents an important Boots brand in its own right. However, research had identified several areas where the existing packaging was not doing justice to the product. To appeal to all types of dieters (crash, long term and healthy eater) the designers identified three areas integral to the upgrading of the original design: the maintenance of a strong brand image, good taste projection and prominent caloric information. They addressed the brand imagery by establishing a systemised design solution, combined with an updated version of the Shapers logo. This system allowed for the display of core information in a coherent pattern with which consumers would become familiar on new products. Good taste projection is achieved by employing photography and illustration in a simple, straightforward fashion where the actual products or ingredients are the heroes of each picture. Caloric information is given due prominence by lifting it out of the body copy into a roundel within the title panel of each product. Displayed in this fashion, consumers can identify the most important dietary information quickly and efficiently.

DESIGN GROUP Newell and Sorrell Ltd
PHOTOGRAPHER Jess Koppel
CLIENT/MANUFACTURER Boots The Chemist

Newell & Sorrell were commissioned to create
a name and packaging for this premium range
of baby foods from Boots. The design employs
a strong blue panel to accentuate Boots'
brand values while atmospheric photography
across the 40 products in the range conveys
the idea of fine ingredients grown using
traditional farming methods. The range forms
part of an overall design strategy for Boots
baby foods. Following its launch, First
Harvest achieved an impressive 5% share
of the UK market in its first year.

CROWTHERS CHRISTMAS RANGE

DESIGNER Karen Welman
ART DIRECTOR Jonathan Ford
ILLUSTRATOR Richard Beards
DESIGN GROUP Pearlfisher International
Design Partnership
CLIENT/MANUFACTURER
Crowthers Restaurant

When Crowthers Restaurant decided to
launch their own range of delicatessen
Christmas puddings, mince pies and
fudge, their brief was to create an identity
conveying gourmet food values within
a festive context. The designers used the
simple idea of illustrating winter
activities, such as sledging and ice skating,
to create 'tracks in the snow'. The overall
effect exploits the unique quality of a simple
white carton. Design details such as
individual booklets and grease-proof wraps
add a distinctive touch to the pack and
deliver a luxurious, quality feel without
the usual festive excess.

HARVEY NICHOLS CHRISTMAS PUDDING

DESIGNERS Stephanie Nash,
Teresa Roviras, Anthony Michael
ART DIRECTORS
Stephanie Nash, Anthony Michael
PHOTOGRAPHER Matthew Donaldson
DESIGN GROUP Michael Nash Associates
CLIENT/MANUFACTURER Harvey Nichols

Following on from the original concept,
thoughts of Christmas evoke childhood
memories of exciting times and being
lucky enough to find the sixpence
hidden in the pudding. This festive
packaging is unique in its sector
and makes a delightful holiday gift.

HARVEY NICHOLS

TRADITIONAL
CHRISTMAS
PUDDING

net
wt. 1lb 454g e

BEST BEFORE: SEE BASE

DESIGN GROUP Dolphin
CLIENT/MANUFACTURER Oliver Peyton

Oliver Peyton commissioned Dolphin to
design the menus for his Piccadilly-based
restaurant. The design was to continue
the 'Atlantic' theme. This was achieved
by featuring different images of crashing
ocean waves supported by a vertical logo
mirroring the way numbers are portrayed
on racing yacht sails.
The use of alternative coloured tints
in the lettering reinforces this imagery.

TLANTIC

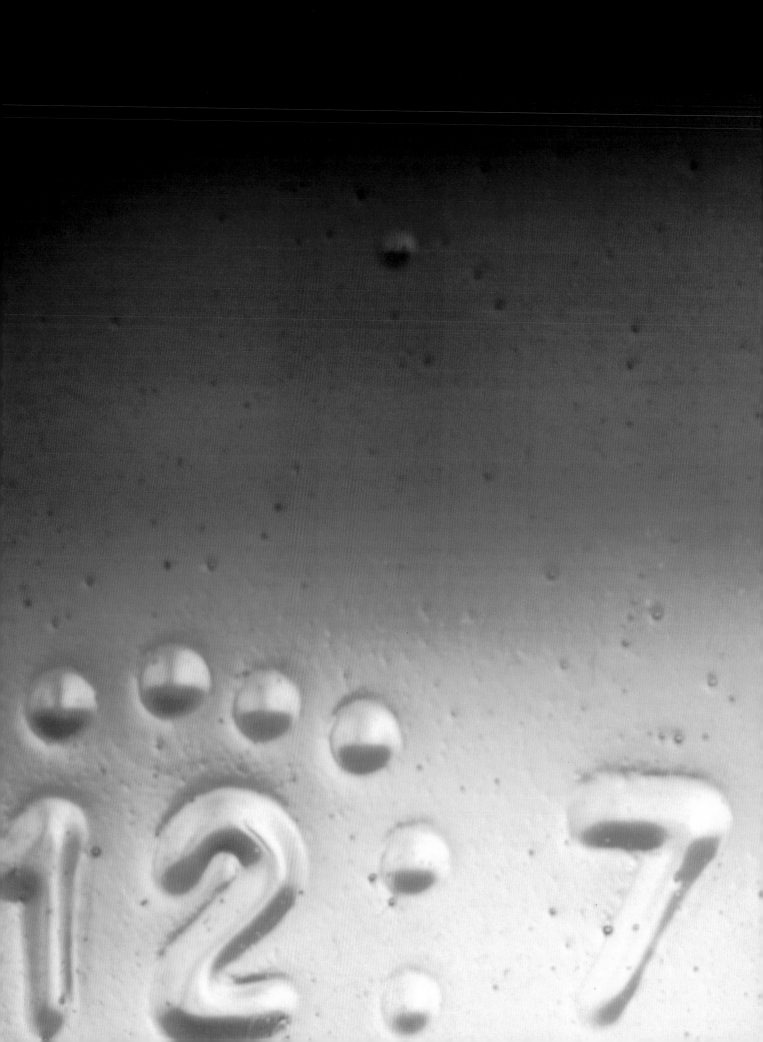

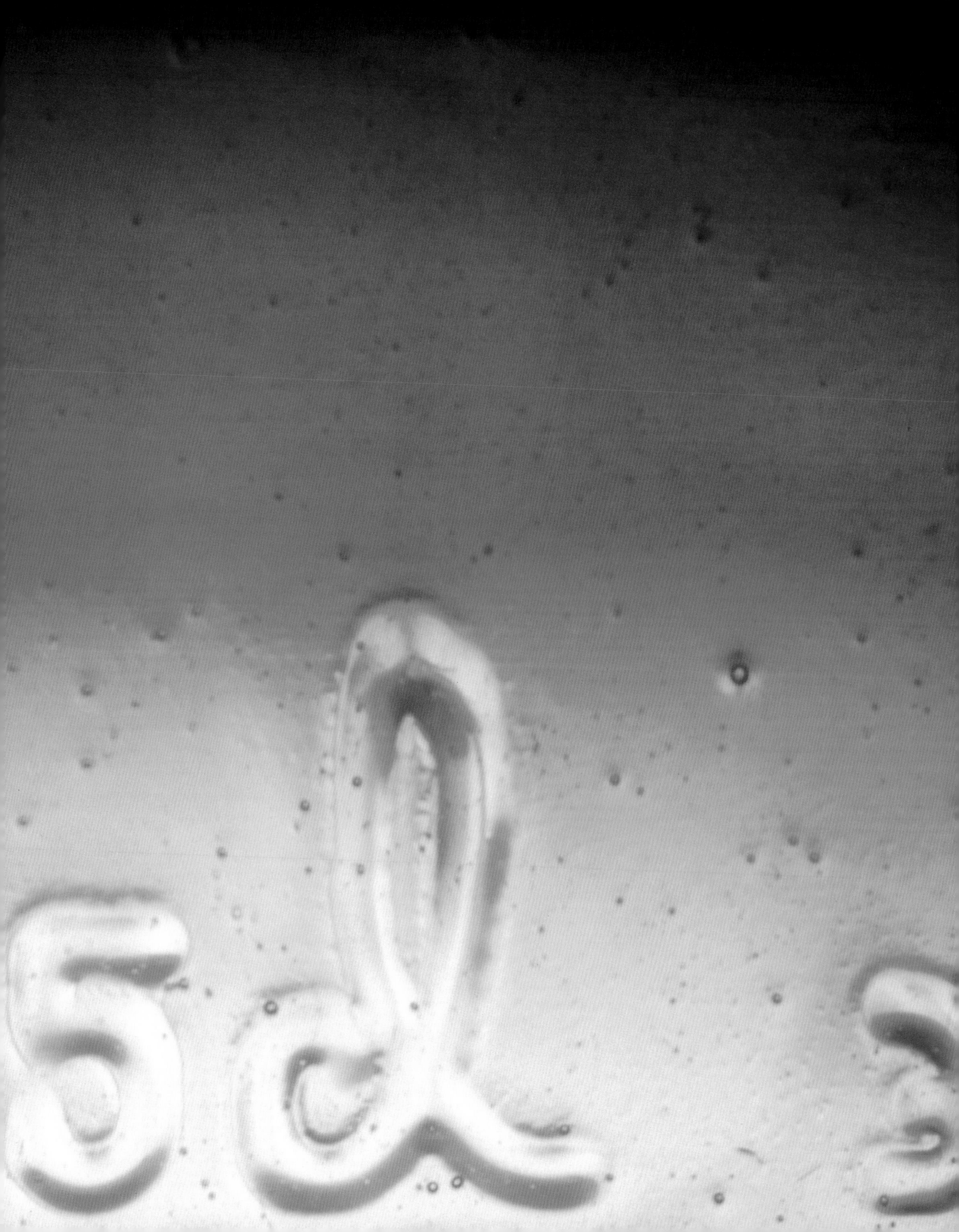

DESIGNER/ART
Director John Blackburn
DESIGN GROUP
Blackburn's Ltd
CLIENT/MANUFACTURER
United Distillers

United Distillers' brief was to create
a distinctive brand identity for Ocumare,
their new rum. It was crucial for the
design to emphasise Ocumare's origins
in the Amazon region, a unique provenance
in a market dominated almost exclusively
by Caribbean rums. It was also important
that the product should stand out as unique
in a market of look-alikes. The brief was
to aim up-market, at a young trendy target
group, for consumption primarily in clubs
rather than for sale in a retail environment.
The chameleon - a creature of the Amazon -
clearly communicates Ocumare's South
American provenance. The uniquely shaped
bottle is also distinctly different to any
other bottle being used by rum distillers.
The chameleon appears as a hologram which,
like the creature, changes colour, creating
a high level of visual excitement and
maximum standout in the product's club/bar
atmosphere. This is believed to be the
first use of a holographic brand identity
on a spirits pack. The chameleon is also
embossed scampering up the back of the
bottle, with its head visible through the big
Ocumare 'O' mnemonic of the front label.

DESIGNER/ART DIRECTOR
John Blackburn
DESIGN GROUP
Blackburn's Ltd
CLIENT/MANUFACTURER
United Distillers

This famous United Distillers brand was given new vitality with a redesign aimed at reinforcing the authenticity and integrity of Pimms.

The 'Empire' panel at the base of the label underlines Pimms' reputation as the drink favoured by high society around the world. It reinforces the prestigious brand values already taken for granted by devotees, and communicates emotively to those consumers new to Pimms.

The new design also enables the brand to compete internationally while preserving its Wimbledon, Ascot and Henley image.

BAILIE NICOL JARVIE BLEND
OLD SCOTCH WHISKY

DESIGNERS
Peter Windett, Wendy Gardiner

ART DIRECTOR
Peter Windett

DESIGN GROUP
Peter Windett & Associates

CLIENT/MANUFACTURER
MacDonald & Muir plc

Here the designers were asked to revise the existing label design for the Bailie Nicol Jarvie Blend of Old Scotch Whisky to re-establish the brand as the premium blended scotch.

A dedicated bottle was used and a second label added to tell the unique story behind the brand. Whilst typographic changes were made and the brand name given more prominence, the eccentric nature of the label was retained.

DESIGNERS
Graham Duffy, Mark Ross
ART DIRECTOR
Graham Duffy
ILLUSTRATOR
Jim Gorman
DESIGN GROUP
Graphic Partners
CLIENT/MANUFACTURER
Glenturret Distillery Ltd

Glenturret Distillery's elegant new liqueur
is a fine example of 'total branding'.
Achieved through the complete integration
of the structural design of the feminine
bottle shape with minimal graphics,
it features decorative paw prints which
create a unique cat motif.

THE GLENROTHES MALT WHISKY

DESIGNER Belinda Duggan
ART DIRECTOR John Blackburn
DESIGN GROUP Blackburn's Ltd
CLIENT/MANUFACTURER
Berry Bros & Rudd Ltd

When Berry Brothers & Rudd commissioned Blackburn's, this malt whisky brand was in trouble. In danger of being delisted, it was losing sales dramatically. Despite several redesigns, the packaging still lacked any individuality, looking as if it had been created to the standard formulae adopted by the whisky market. The objective was to give The Glenrothes a radical and individual identity. The idea for the new design came from the Taster's Sample Room in the distillery.

The bottle shape and the discrete hand-signed half-label communicate the integrity and authenticity of the malt. The presentation carton is similarly un-embellished, with the Royal Warrant giving the product a further prestige endorsement. Instead of 'twelve-year-old malt', the label gives the whisky's year of distillation. The highly distinctive identity 'the malt with the simple label' now makes The Glenrothes a unique individual whisky, out-performing competitors at a similar price.

The design has enhanced the impression of quality and integrity. Sales have increased by more than 200%, with new listings including, for the first time, international duty free outlets. The brand's fortunes have been transformed by the new packaging, with no advertising support.

COCKBURN'S SPECIAL RESERVE GIFT CARTON

DESIGNER Belinda Duggan
ART DIRECTOR John Blackburn
ILLUSTRATOR Unichrome Ltd
DESIGN GROUP Blackburn's Ltd
CLIENT/MANUFACTURER
Cockburn Smithes & Cia Ltd

Blackburn's first designed the Cockburn's
Special Reserve bottle 25 years ago. More
recently, Cockburn's needed a special gift
carton suitable for Christmas and year-round
sales. The carton design had to reflect and
reinforce Cockburn's Special Reserve's unique
properties as an accessible port, suitable
for anyone to enjoy. The design features
the Cockburn's cockerel - the brand's symbol
for many years - drinking a glass of Special
Reserve Port. He can be seen in successive

images around the sides of the carton, sipping
it down gently. In one image he's caught red-
faced. The idea expresses the brand's populist
proposition and its advertising line 'Always
special ... so why reserve it?' as a graphic
joke. The witty style and red colours also help
to reflect Cockburn's Special Reserve's
personality and its image as the accessible
port brand. The image has a festive feel for
Christmas, but is equally relevant for sales
at any time of the year.

HARVEY'S BRISTOL CREAM

DESIGNER/ART
Director John Blackburn
DESIGN GROUP
Blackburn's Ltd
CLIENT/MANUFACTURER
Allied Domecq / Harvey's of Bristol

The redesign of Harvey's Bristol Cream
was prompted by a serious decline in
sales and brand share. Not only was
Bristol Cream losing its status as a
premium brand and being overtaken by
own-label sherries, it was also perceived
as outdated and unappealing. To recover
its status, it had to encourage people
to drink sherry more often than just
at Christmas, weddings or funerals.
The whole sector needed to be revitalised
before cream sherry faced its own funeral.
The challenge called for a radical change.
The idea is simple and, as so often, seems
obvious: put Bristol Cream into Bristol
Blue glass, thus harnessing the distinctive
cobalt blue glass, which has been specific
to Bristol for more than two centuries,
to the Harvey's name, which has been
synonymous with Bristol for just as long.
The established Harvey's 'keystone' label,
the only element retained from the old
design, has been given a fresh treatment.
The blue bottle is highly distinctive
in a market of brown and green bottles.
The colour has become a unique equity
and provides the big idea behind subsequent
brand promotions designed to rebuild
Harvey's Bristol Cream. The design has
also greatly increased the brand's appeal
to younger drinkers. Since the launch
of the new design, consumer sales have
increased by 16%, the brand has taken
a 6% lead and the overall market has
seen new dynamism, with considerable
growth for the whole sector.

DESIGNER/ART DIRECTOR
Mary Lewis
DESIGN GROUP
Lewis Moberly
CLIENT/MANUFACTURER
Arnold Dettling

Typically, kirsch is a colourless liquid
packaged in clear flint standard bottles.
Leading Swiss brand Dettling's brief was
to break the mould and design a unique
bottle. The designer took the opportunity
to create a radically different presentation
within the category.
The design takes its inspiration from the
Black Cherry itself. The coloured glass
reflects the deep stain of the fruit.
The slim bottle has a flat back and curved
front with an applied label only on the neck.
The brand's credentials are in hand-drawn
clear script against a frosted surface.

DESIGNER/ART DIRECTOR Katie Bergin
ILLUSTRATOR John See
DESIGN GROUP Curious
CLIENT/MANUFACTURER Cadenheads

This design was commissioned by Cadenheads, a renowned bottler of malt whiskies. Their Covent Garden Unique Blend Whisky is stocked exclusively at the Cadenheads Covent Garden Whisky Shop. As such, it is aimed at a tourist trade looking for a whisky with authenticity and heritage, but with a relevance and accessibility to them. Since many tourists may not have included a visit to Scotland in their trip, the brief was to produce a design that combined traditional whisky values but which, instead of focusing on Scotland, drew on the heritage and fashionable imagery of Covent Garden. The work needed a souvenir-like quality to give the Covent Garden Blend high-quality perceptions and almost ornamental values. The label design depicts the sociability of the people of Covent Garden through the ages, moving from the days of Victorian romance, through the famous fruit and vegetable market, the business meeting area and on to street-theatre. The gold foil blocked wrap-around illustration takes in the famous view of Covent Garden, moving from the Church across the piazza back to the Church. The bottles are all batch-numbered by hand to add further premium values.

ASDA HUNGARIAN WINES

DESIGNER Gary Swindell
PHOTOGRAPHER Simon Larbelestier
DESIGN GROUP Elmwood Design
CLIENT/MANUFACTURER Asda Stores

This design solution supports Asda's philosophy for their wines, which is to maintain a distinctive quality look while pioneering creativity of presentation within the overall wine sector. The key aim for this range of wines was to appeal to the younger, experimental wine drinkers looking for something innovative and different.

The challenge was to provide a creative proposition which positioned Hungarian wines alongside Asda's New World wines. Hungarian wine is relatively new to the UK and so could be viewed as a modern wine alongside the New World products. However, Hungary has an old European culture, so the design solution had to project a new from old image. The use of old Hungarian folk tales to inspire images rendered in a modern manner provided the perfect solution and enabled the range to dovetail into Asda's overall wine strategy.

DESIGNERS Chen Tsoi, Kara Sims
ART DIRECTOR Chen Tsoi
ILLUSTRATOR Matthew Cooper
DESIGN GROUP Chen Tsoi Design
CLIENT/MANUFACTURER Tesco Stores Ltd

When Tesco introduced South African wines
to their New World wine category their brief
called for the production of a new genre
of wine label. Emphasis was to be put on
the fact that the wine was very different,
and originating from South Africa. Chen Tsoi
used a rich, colour-ful style of illustration,
covering the whole label, to depict various
aspects of South Africa. The main copy
was held in a coloured block matched by
the neck label. The design of the range
was extended by the different colour coding
of the neck label and the copy panel.

DESIGNER Belinda Duggan
ART DIRECTOR John Blackburn
ILLUSTRATOR Bob Pattini
Design Group Blackburn's Ltd
CLIENT/MANUFACTURER
Cockburn Smithes & Cia Ltd

Cockburn's brief was to design a label
which would help people understand
Quinta Vintage Port, thus demystifying
this traditionally exclusive sector.
The strategy was to reflect and continue
Cockburn's mission of making port
accessible. The roadsign icons on the
label communicate complex product
information in a simple way, without
being patronising. The overall look
remains understated, classic and stylish.
An exclusive product is thus made
accessible without losing its status.

ART DIRECTOR
Simon Pemberton
DESIGNERS
Simon Pemberton, Adrian Whitefoord
ILLUSTRATORS
Gilly Lovegrove, Linda Jeffries
DESIGN GROUP
Pemberton & Whitefoord
CLIENT/MANUFACTURER
Victoria Wines

This brief called for the creation of
a credible offering from Argentina,
a country with little wine heritage
in the UK market. The design combines
classical hand-drawn typography with
fresh bold, colourful illustrations of
typical features of the Mendoza region.
The use of these illustrations enabled
the wines to compete with the existing
New World wines already on the
market, allowing them to stand out
in a particularly crowded sector.

HARVEY'S GRAN SOLERA

DESIGNER
Belinda Duggan
ART DIRECTOR
John Blackburn
ILLUSTRATOR
John Geary
DESIGN GROUP
Blackburn's Ltd
CLIENT/MANUFACTURER
Allied Domecq / Harvey's of Bristol

The objective here was to communicate
the prestige of this high quality
old Oloroso sherry, which is sold only
in duty-free outlets. The Carthusian
horse, spirited and pure-bred, forms
a logo symbolising the rarity and
breeding of Gran Solera sherry.
The carton has subtle two-tone colour
values, with front and back faces in
black and the sides in a very dark blue
relevant to Gran Solera's sophisticated
personality. The embossed logo
in raised gold and the velvet ribbon
which adorns the carton also underline
the brand's prestige.

DESIGNERS
Eddie Turley, Don Williams
CREATIVE DIRECTOR
Don Williams
DESIGN GROUP
P.I. Design International
CLIENT/MANUFACTURER
Matthew Clark plc

Matthew Clark's brief called for the
development of a new brand name,
identity and bottle for a totally
colourless cider designed to appeal
to eighteen to twenty-five-year-olds
of both sexes. The solution emphasises
Vox's unique transparent quality by
asking the consumer to actually look
through the product. The brand name
is printed on the front of the bottle
seen against a black circle. The circle
is, in fact, a distortion created by an
oval shape on the back of the bottle.
As the bottle moves, so the design
changes shape.

PERNOD HEX

DESIGNER
Karen Welman, Leyton Hardwick
ART DIRECTOR
Karen Welman
DESIGN GROUP
Pearlfisher International
Design Partnership
CLIENT/MANUFACTURER
Campbell Distillers Ltd

In the crowded drinks market aimed at the
club-goer it's hard to be original. Pernod's
distinctive heritage was key to the creation
of this new identity as a ready-mixed cocktail.
The name Pernod Hex, meaning Witches' brew,
was chosen to reflect the unusual nature of
the parent and the potency of the offspring,
designed to compete in the style-conscious
club scene. The graphics are strong and
stylish, hinting at the brand's heritage, and
by using a classic beer structure the cocktail
is given real 'street cred.'

Designer/Art Director
Roger Akroyd
DESIGN GROUP
Michael Peters Ltd
CLIENT/MANUFACTURER
Brasserie du Cardinal Fribourg

Cardinal is a leading brand in the
Swiss drinks market. In common
with its domestic competitors,
it is losing out to imported beers
with more relevance to younger
drinkers. Michael Peters Limited's
task was to develop a new concept
to launch the first cold filtration
lager in the market.
MPL customised existing bottle
shapes by embossing them with
the name and used the Cardinal
branding and graphics to create
a unique positioning statement.

On the label (shown upside-down in the image):

P1960

This unique and ingenious new system

give you the smooth, less bitter taste

DRAUGHT

and creamy head of draught Murphy's.

DRAUGHTFLOW · SYSTEM

MURPHY'S IRISH STOUT

DESIGNER
Torben Dunn
ART DIRECTOR
Ian Ritchie
DESIGN GROUP
Jones Knowles Ritchie
CLIENT/MANUFACTURER
Murphy's Brewery Ireland

Guinness, the brand leader in the market
for Irish stout, has a clear identity known
throughout the British Isles. Murphy's brief
to the designers was to produce an identity
for a creditable competitor without running
the risk of looking like an also-ran.
The cream in the design reflects the essential
qualities of the product while the graphics
convey images of its heritage and tradition.

BLACK SHEEP ALE

DESIGNER
Simon Coker

ART DIRECTOR
Mark Wickens

LETTERING ARTIST
Peter Horridge

ILLUSTRATOR
Anton Morris

DESIGN GROUP
Wickens Tutt Southgate

CLIENT/MANUFACTURER
Black Sheep Brewery Ltd

Having lost the family firm to Scottish & Newcastle, Paul Theakston became disillusioned with the new owner and chose to start again alone. He regards himself as the black sheep of the family for having sold the firm in the first place, hence the name of his first brand. This real ale was therefore intentionally positioned as a maverick; a personality which was masculine, self-assured, fiercely independent yet sociable. The target audience is broad, from knowledgeable real ale drinkers to younger premium lager drinkers. The design solution needed to encapsulate all the traditions and dark visual language of strong real ale, but with an interesting new twist. The brand is the hero. It is, indeed, literally a brand in every sense, appearing to have been tamped directly onto the sheep. Overtly masculine and strong, it has an underlying humour with a distinctive quirk.

DESIGNER/ART DIRECTOR
Darrell Ireland
DESIGN GROUP
The Foundry Design Consultants Ltd
CLIENT/MANUFACTURER
Waitrose

This porter is new to Waitrose, with
nothing like it sold in-store before.
A cross between a beer and a stout,
porter was extremely popular many
years ago. It is enjoying a revival
among brewers and the real ale
drinkers who enjoy these specialist
beers. The designers were asked
to convey these traditional elements
through a new label design.
The inspiration came from the image
of lights shining through the stained
glass windows of public houses at
night. The designers wanted to capture
the warm, glowing elements and vivid
colour of the stained glass.
Harry Willock's illustration combined
with Darrell Ireland's hand lettering
provided the perfect image for this
new porter.

MARSTON'S HEAD BREWER'S CHOICE BEERS

DESIGNER Jo Brock
ART DIRECTOR Ian Ritchie
DESIGN GROUP Jones Knowles Ritchie
CLIENT/MANUFACTURER Marston's Brewery

Guest beers generate customer traffic in pubs
and thus present profit opportunities.
Marston's brief to Jones Knowles Ritchie was
to create a system which would make it easy
to introduce a guest beer on a month by month
basis. The solution is a fixed counter-mount
highlighting the umbrella branding 'Marston's
Head Brewer's Choice' with each guest beer
featured on a separate metal plaque clipped
onto the counter-mount. Each plaque is
designed to reflect its beer's specific heritage
and can be passed on from pub to pub within
the Marston's group. This simple design
solution has turned a logistical problem into
a profitable opportunity.

DUBONNET CAN

DESIGNERS Karen Welman, Kate Barsby
ART DIRECTOR Jonathan Ford
DESIGN GROUP Pearlfisher International
Design Partnership
CLIENT/MANUFACTURER Campbell Distillers Ltd

The release of this new premixed version
of Dubonnet in a can was intended firstly
to recruit a younger audience and secondly
to make the product appear lighter and
fresher than the standard bottle. Research
indicated that the popular perception of
the parent brand was that it was rather
outdated. It was thus imperative to
represent Dubonnet in a way significantly
different to the standard bottle, but
without losing its valuable heritage.
The designers' solution was to revive
the simple Cassandre illustration,
and re-emphasise the type, removing
many of the cluttered elements to
arrive at a simpler execution.
None of the brand's authenticity
is lost in this striking new version.

DESIGNER
Torben Dunn
ART DIRECTOR
Ian Ritchie
DESIGN GROUP
Jones Knowles Ritchie
CLIENT/MANUFACTURER
The Whitbread Beer Company Ltd

This new identity for Whitbread Best
Bitter is an evolved treatment of an
established image, designed to restate
the brand's image as a contemporary
classic. Much of the emphasis of
the design relies on a reiteration of
traditional brewing images: the brewer's
signature, hops and strong typography.

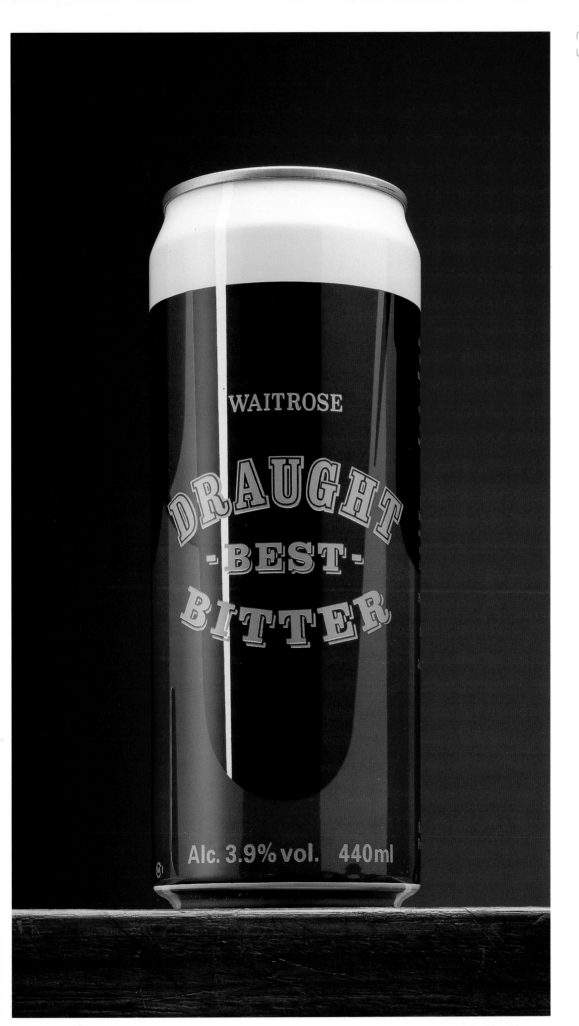

DESIGNERS
Darrell Ireland, Melanie Ryan
ART DIRECTOR
Darrell Ireland
DESIGN GROUP
The Foundry Design Consultants Ltd
CLIENT/MANUFACTURER
Waitrose

The Foundry's solution to this problem - making the can look like a glass of beer - looked simple on paper. The trompe l'oeil effect was much harder to achieve in reality, but was highly successful and effective after many days of trial and error. A number of concepts were presented to the client for this product. To the designers' surprise, the most adventurous idea was chosen, allowing for a conceptually strong design that is completely unique in its sector.

DESIGNER
John Ewles
ART DIRECTOR
Ian Ritchie
DESIGN GROUP
Jones Knowles Ritchie
CLIENT/MANUFACTURER
Marston's Brewery

New advertising, reciprocal distribution deals and an enhanced brand identity have been moving Marston's Pedigree on from its market position in its regional heartland to that of a premium national brand. In creating its new identity, the designers had to be aware of the need to offer the right kind of aspirational values to new customers whilst retaining credibility with the brand's established regular drinkers. Through its simple graphics, bright colours and high-quality finish, the pint bottle presents a fine balance between modernity and heritage.

DESIGNERS
Darrell Ireland, Melanie Ryan
ART DIRECTOR
Darrell Ireland
DESIGN GROUP
The Foundry Design Consultants Ltd
CLIENT/MANUFACTURER
Waitrose

This own-brand lager had to establish its own identity and compete with all the other branded products sold by the client. The lager is a very high strength product, and this was to be emphasized in the graphic approach. To signal this, the designers decided on a bright red background for its immediate standout and the way it issues a 'warning' to the customer that they are dealing with a very intoxicating drink. All the remaining information was positioned within the rings of a target.
The VSL monogram acts as a suitable central motif to offset the design, and adds that extra touch of individuality and authenticity.

DESIGNERS Tim Perkins,
Daniel Cornell, Paul Browton
ART DIRECTOR Tim Perkins
DESIGN GROUP Design Bridge Ltd
CLIENT/MANUFACTURER Bass Brewers Ltd

Following a market shift away from
regional ales, Bass nominated
Worthington as their national brand
for 1996. This created a need
to reposition the brand to attract
a younger market without alienating
the regional core loyalists, mainly
found in South Wales. Research
indicated that consumers found
the existing design old-fashioned,
cluttered and with few recognisable
brand equities. The first task was
to review the hierarchy of
communication. 'Draught' is key
and therefore emphasised, whereas
'Best' is no longer meaningful.
The designers retained the red
'hotspot', but with a less obtrusive
interpretation of the shield device.
The Worthington name retains its
heroic qualities, but with
a rejuvenated type-face to reflect
youthfulness and dynamism.
The green background, the one key
equity, was also retained.
The creamflow technology Bass is
now employing across all its brands,
to deliver a creamier pint, is
reflected in the flowing logo which
allows for repeat branding on the shelf.

DESIGNER
Paul Davies
ART DIRECTOR
David Wombwell
DESIGN GROUP
Ziggurat
CLIENT/MANUFACTURER
Spendrup's of Sweden

Major Swedish brewer Spendrup's rose rapidly to success during the 1980s boom. Privately owned, the company made its name as the successful and popular 'private alternative' to the state-owned brewing monopoly. Its corporate identity suggested all the surface glamour of that entrepreneurial era. But the 1990s brought a new perspective; the old image had lost relevance in a market increasingly crowded with foreign imports, mostly sporting the credible 'real beer' imagery of heritage, tradition and craft. Unable to share these values, Spendrup's simple promise of great-tasting beer was not enough.

This new brand identity restates the company's genuine brewing credentials, with a strong new emphasis on family tradition. The founding forefathers are given a leading role, framed within twin heroic medallions. Luxuriant swags of hops and barley underpin the branding to communicate the firm's commitment to traditional craft techniques and exclusively natural ingredients.

The identity aims to distil an essence of 'Old Sweden' into a single graphic image, thus giving drinkers reason to believe in the attractive idea of a quality Swedish speciality. The new branding has been implemented as a corporate identity covering stationery, vehicles, signage and retail merchandising.

DESIGNERS
Brian Green, James Bell
ART DIRECTOR
Judi Green
DESIGN GROUP
The Green House
CLIENT/MANUFACTURER
Löwenbräu Ltd

Löwenbräu UK Limited, a wholly
owned subsidiary of Löwenbräu AG
(Munich), wanted to reposition and
revitalise their Premium Bier range
to take advantage of the strong
growth in the premium sector.
The new designs aim to reclaim
Löwenbräu's original position as
an authentic, premium, good quality
beer and communicate the heritage
of the brew in a uniform and
focused way. The overall task was
to introduce consistency across the
range and communicate authority,
heritage and authenticity whilst
encouraging the reappraisal of
the brand as a really good German
premium beer. The packaging
communicates the key benefit of
quality whilst clarifying the brand's
German heritage and tradition.

CARLING BLACK LABEL
SPECIAL EDITION PACK

DESIGNER Garrick Hamm
ART DIRECTOR Glenn Tutssel
ILLUSTRATOR Colin Frewin
DESIGN GROUP Tutssels
CLIENT/MANUFACTURER Bass

Carling Black Label's Special Edition
can links the brand with its sponsorship
of premiership football. The new
packaging created unprecedented demand
from trade and consumers alike during
the two-month period that the product
was available, and won the 1995 Design
Effectiveness award in the branded food
and drink category.

DESIGNER Nick Hanson
ART DIRECTOR Glenn Tutssel
DESIGN GROUP Tutssels
CLIENT/MANUFACTURER Bass

The designers' brief was to give
the Tennent's 500ml Pilsner
can highershelf standout against
its competitors in the mainstream
lager market, to move the design
away from other brands in the
portfolio to prevent cannibalisation
and to increase the brand's share
in the value-for-money sector of
this large market.
Using the red and white colourway,
the can is designed to build on the
lager's Czech brewing origins and
reflect its light, youthful brand
values. It was important to evolve
the design without bringing it into
conflict with the existing counter-
mount or alienating existing Pilsner
drinkers. The designers created
an identity which has strong impact
and the potential to create a clear
brand section at the point of
purchase. The design has both
increased visibility and distanced
the brand from the other Tennant's
line extensions.

SUPERBOCK SEASONAL PACK

DESIGNER Daniel Cornell
ART DIRECTOR Keren House
PHOTOGRAPHER David Gill
DESIGN GROUP Design Bridge Ltd
Client/Manufacturer Unicer

Superbock is Portugal's leading beer.
With a market share of over 45%, it is
backed by continuous advertising and
promotional activity directed towards
its consumers.
Design Bridge were asked to develop a
range of themed, seasonal multi-packs
celebrating, in this case, Easter. Their
solution positions the characteristic
red oval of Superbock amongst the
decorative painted eggs featured at this
time of religious and popular celebration.

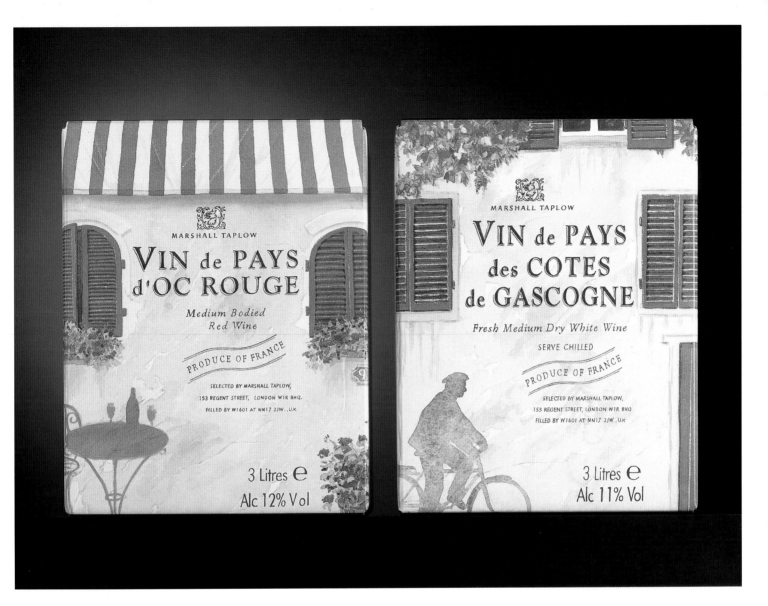

DESIGNER Simon Pemberton
ART DIRECTORS Simon Pemberton,
Adrian Whitefoord
DESIGN GROUP Pemberton & Whiteford
CLIENT/MANUFACTURER Marshall Taplow

The brief here was to resurrect a dying
brand through a major packaging relaunch.
The design reflects the nature and proposition
of the wine, with the use of fresh, lively
watercolour illustrations of typical French
everyday genres.
The hand-drawn typography was used to
create a trompe l'oeil effect on the boxes.
Combined with the illustrations, the wine
boxes become a French café and house.
The illustrations' monochromatic colour
themes are used for product differentiation.
The design results in a strong range identity
in the store while still allowing each wine
its own individuality.

AGENDA DESIGN ASSOCIATES
IMA House
20 Northfields
London SW18 1PE
Tel: 0181 870 1847
Fax: 0181 870 7517
Contact: Paul Davis

BEN DRURY & WILLIAM BANKHEAD
142D Tachbrook Street
London SW1V 2NE
Tel: 0171 834 6218
Fax: 0171 834 6218
Contact: Ben Drury

BLACKBURN'S LIMITED
16 Carlisle Street
London W1V 5RE
Tel: 0171 734 7646
Fax: 0171 437 0017
Contact: Isabel Collins

CARTER WONG AND PARTNERS
29 Brook Mews North
London W2 3BW
Tel: 0171 224 9139
Fax: 0171 402 4122
email: cwpart@mail.bogo.co.uk
Contact: Philip Carter

CDT DESIGN LIMITED
21 Brownlow Mews
London WC1N 2LA
Tel: 0171 242 0992
Fax: 0171 242 1174
Contact: Claire Robinson

CHEN TSOI DESIGN
87 Arlington Road
London NW1 7ES
Tel: 0171 383 0185
Fax: 0171 383 0186
Contact: Chen Tsoi

CHRISSIE CHARLTON & COMPANY
Nile Street Studios
8 Nile Street
London N1 7RF
Tel: 0171 251 2170
Fax: 0171 251 2145
Contact: Chrissie Charlton

CLARKS INTERNATIONAL
40 High Street
Street
Somerset BA16 0YA
Tel: 01458 443 131
Fax: 01458 840 996
Contact: Ian Wills

COLEY PORTER BELL
11A West Halkin Street
London SW1X 8JL
Tel: 0171 470 4000
Fax: 0171 470 4001
email: admin@cpb.u-net.com
Contact: Brendan Martin

CURIOUS
6 Dean Street
London W1V 5RN
Tel: 0171 734 4585
Fax: 0171 734 4586
email: curious@easynet.co.uk
Contact: Philip Baker, Graham Hales

DAVID RICHMOND ASSOCIATES
3 Northington Street
London WC1N 2JE
Tel: 0171 831 4828
Fax: 0171 242 1055
Contact: Dave Richmond

DAVIES HALL
The Forum
74-80 Camden Street
London NW1 0EG
Tel: 0171 387 7112
Fax: 0171 387 3454
Contact: George Sugden

DED ASSOCIATES
The Workstation
15 Paternoster Row
Sheffield
South Yorkshire S1 2BX
Tel: 0114 249 3939
Fax: 0114 249 3940
email: design@dedass.demon.co.uk
Contact: Nik Daughtry

DELANEY DESIGN CONSULTANTS
10 Whitehorse Mews
Westminster Bridge Road
London SE1 7QD
Tel: 0171 401 7788
Fax: 0171 401 3388
Contact: Brian Delaney

DESIGN BRIDGE LIMITED
18 Clerkenwell Close
London EC1R 0AA
Tel: 0171 814 9922
Fax: 0171 814 9024
Contact: Liz Ramsay

DIN GRAPHICS
32 St. Oswald's Place
London SE11 5JE
Tel: 0171 582 0777
Fax: 0171 582 3080
Contact: Valerie Wickes

DOLPHIN
32 Neal Street
London WC2H 9PS
Tel: 0171 379 5671
Fax: 0171 497 9121
Contact: Sasha Castling

ELMWOOD
Ghyll Royd
Guiseley
Leeds LS20 9LT
Tel: 01943 870 229
Fax: 01943 870 191
email: wow!@elmwood.co.uk
Contact: Greg Taylor

FARRINGTON ASSOCIATES
Fourth Floor
193 Wardour Street
London W1V 3FA
Tel: 0171 434 3346
Fax: 0171 734 5097
Contact: Sammy Farrington

FLUID
1/106 The Custard Factory
Gibb Street
Birmingham B9 4AA
Tel: 0121 693 6913
Fax: 0121 693 6913
email: drop@fluid.custard.co.uk
web site: http://www.custard.co.uk/fluid/
Contact: James Glover, Neil Roddis

THE FOUNDRY DESIGN CONSULTANTS LTD
10E Printing House Yard
Hackney Road
London E2 7PR
Tel: 0171 739 4512
Fax: 0171 729 7278
Contact: Darrell Ireland

GRAPHIC PARTNERS
Gladstone Court
179 Canongate
Edinburgh EH8 8BN
Tel: 0131 557 3558
Fax: 0131 558 1430
Contact: Claire Whyte, Graham Duffy

THE GREEN HOUSE
64 High Street
Harrow-on-the-Hill
Middlesex
London HA1 3LL
Tel: 0181 422 6178
Fax: 0181 864 8370
Contact: Judi Green

GREENWICH DESIGN ASSOCIATES
David Mews
11A Greenwich South Street
London SE10 8NW
Tel: 0181 853 3028
Fax: 0181 858 2128
Contact: Simon Wright, Lynn McKenna

HORSEMAN COOKE
32-37 Cowper Street
London EC2A 4AP
Tel: 0171 251 0588
Fax: 0171 251 0782
email: horsecooke@atlas.co.uk
Contact: Mike Horseman

HUTTON & PARTNERS
5 Apollo Studios
Charlton Kings Road
London NW5 2SB
Tel: 0171 482 2140
Fax: 0171 485 6068
Contact: Stephen Hutton

IAN LOGAN DESIGN COMPANY
42 Charterhouse Square
London EC1 MGEU
Tel: 0171 606 1803
Fax: 0171 726 6419
Contact: Ian Logan

JONES KNOWLES RITCHIE
The Rotunda
42-43 Gloucester Crescent
London NW1 7DL
Tel: 0171 284 3878
Fax: 0171 284 3879
Contact: Andy Knowles, Julie Crothswaite

LANDOR ASSOCIATES
Klamath House
18 Clerkenwell Green
London EC1R 0DP
Tel: 0171 880 8000
Fax: 0171 880 8001
email: david-redhill@landor.com
Contact: David Redhill

LEWIS MOBERLY
33 Gresse Street
London W1P 2LP
Tel: 0171 580 9252
Fax: 0171 255 1671
Contact: Jo Maude

LIGHT & COLEY INTERNATIONAL
20 Fulham Broadway
London SW6 1AH
Tel: 0171 381 6644
Fax: 0171 381 2833
Contact: Alan Coley

LIPPA PEARCE DESIGN LTD

358A Richmond Road

London TW1 2DU

Tel: 0181 744 2100

Fax: 0181 744 2770

Contact: Domenic Lippa

THE LONDON DESIGN PARTNERSHIP LTD

6 Great Queen Street

London WC2B 5DG

Tel: 0171 430 2939

Fax: 0171 430 1488

Contact: Barbara J Lewis

LYDIA THORNLEY

Shoreditch Studio

44-46 Scrutton Street

London EC2A 4HH

Tel: 0171 377 2777

Fax: 0171 377 5439

email: http://www.poptel.org.uk/hackney-business/lydia-thornley/.

Contact: Lydia Thornley

MICHAEL NASH ASSOCIATES

42-44 Newman Street

London W1P 3PA

Tel: 0171 631 3370

Fax: 0171 637 9629

Contact: Wendy Gilliatt

MICHAEL PETERS LIMITED

49 Princes Place

London W11 4QA

Tel: 0171 229 3424

Fax: 0171 221 7720

email: brands@mpldesign.co.uk

Contact: Julie McDowell

MILLER SUTHERLAND

6 D'Arblay Street

London W1V 3FD

Tel: 0171 437 2901

Fax: 0171 734 6028

Contact: Sian Sutherland

MINALE, TATTERSFIELD & PARTNERS LIMITED

The Courtyard

37 Sheen Road

Richmond

Surrey TW9 1AJ

Tel: 0181 948 7999

Fax: 0181 948 2435

email: mintat@cityscape.co.uk

Contact: Lizah Honey

NETTLE DESIGN LIMITED

'O' Warehouse

Metropolitan Wharf

Wapping Wall

London E1 9SS

Tel: 0171 265 0957

Fax: 0171 702 0506

Contact: John Hurst

NEWELL AND SORRELL LIMITED

4 Utopia Village

Chalcot Road

London NW1 8LH

Tel: 0171 722 1113

Fax: 0171 722 0259

Contact: Jeremy Scholfield

PEARLFISHER INTERNATIONAL DESIGN PARTNERSHIP

12 Addison Avenue

Holland Park

London W11 4QR

Tel: 0171 603 8666

Fax: 0171 603 1208

Contact: Paul Cowper

PEMBERTON AND WHITEFOORD

25 Plympton Street

London NW8 8AB

Tel: 0171 723 8899

Fax: 0171 723 6131

Contact: S. Pemberton

PENTAGRAM DESIGN LIMITED

11 Needham Road

London W11 2RP

Tel: 0171 229 3477

Fax: 0171 727 9932

email: email@pentagram.co.uk

Contact: Julia Wyatt

PETER WINDETT & ASSOCIATES

55-57 South Edwardes Square

London W8 6HP

Tel: 0171 221 0301

Fax: 0171 602 6545

Contact: Peter Windett

P. I. DESIGN INTERNATIONAL

1-5 Colville Mews

Lonsdale Road

London W11 2AR

Tel: 0171 727 3226

Fax: 0171 727 4831

Contact: Chantel Bordet

ROUNDEL DESIGN GROUP

7 Rosehart Mews

Westbourne Grove

London W11 3TY

Tel: 0171 221 1951

Fax: 0171 221 1843

Contact: John Bateson

SHIEL/HUMPHREY DESIGN

1 Northfields Prospect

Putney Bridge Road

London SW18 1HX

Tel: 0181 874 2408

Fax: 0181 874 7765

email: 74212.727.@compuserve.com

Contact: Tricia Shiel, Jonathan Humphrey

Shiel/Humphrey (USA)

4125 Ibis Street

San Diego

California 92103

Tel: (001) 619 543 0845

Fax: (001) 619 543 0038

SMITH & BULL LIMITED

The Guardship

Church Street

London W4 2PH

Tel: 0181 742 8383

Fax: 0181 742 8118

email: studio@smifbull.demon.co.uk

Contact: Alex or Louise

SMITH & MILTON ORIGINAL

Boatmen's Institution

27 Junction Mews

London W2 1PN

Tel: 0171 706 1414

Fax: 0171 706 1313

Contact: Howard Milton

SPRINGETT ASSOCIATES

13 Salisbury Place

London W1H 1FJ

Tel: 0171 486 7527

Fax: 0171 487 3033

email: 101565.3470@compuserve uk

Contact: Kate Killeen, Peter Green

SYSTEM GAFA

13 Stoney Street

London SE1 9AD

Tel: 0171 403 7067

Fax: 0171 403 7067

Contact: Yuki Miyake

TRICKETT & WEBB LIMITED

The Factory

84 Marchmont Street

London WC1N 1AG

Tel: 0171 388 5832

Fax: 0171 387 4287

email: brian@tricketts.co.uk

Contact: Brian Webb

TURNER DUCKWORTH

Voysey House

Barley Mow Passage

London W4 4PH

Tel: 0181 994 7190

Fax: 0181 994 7192

Contact: Bruce Duckworth, Chris Collis

Turner Duckworth (USA)

665 Third Avenue, Suite 509

San Francisco

California

Tel: (001) 415 495 8691

Fax: (001) 415 495 8692

Contact: David Turner

TUTSSELS

48 Beak Street

London W1R 3DA

Tel: 0171 753 8466

Fax: 0171 434 1098

email: tutssels@dial pipex.com

Contact: Liz Dunning, Helen Owen

WICKENS TUTT SOUTHGATE

10A Frederick Close

London W2 2HD

Tel: 0171 262 1707

Fax: 0171 262 1512

Contact: Mark Wickens

ZIGGURAT

20 Chenies Street

London WC1E 7EX

Tel: 0171 636 9966

Fax: 0171 255 1187

Contact: David Wombwell